paper

Designs by
Jeanette Bakker, Jill Elias,
Helen Roberts Hill, Jean Riley,
and Marie Waterhouse

THUNDER BAY
P·R·E·S·S
San Diego, California

contents

techniques

projects

Introduction

Paper is such a common material that we take it for granted. It is in daily use in newspapers and packaging, as writing paper, and for computer printouts. Apart from such utilitarian uses, it also serves as a surface for many artistic endeavors, including drawing, painting, printmaking, and three-dimensional work.

Dr. Allen Stevenson, in the introduction to Charles Briquet's *Opuscula, Helversum* (Paper Publications Society, 1955), stated that "after meat and wood and possibly aspirin, paper may well be man's most important commodity. Its force has been more subtle and far reaching than anything else at all except the spirit of man, and except print itself, which has no meaning, no existence without a printing surface."

Before the advent of paper, there were a number of both rigid and flexible predecessors; for example, clay and wax tablets, papyrus, and similar materials made from plants. The most durable but expensive writing material was vellum, which was made from animal skins. Paper, particularly after the invention of the printing press, revolutionized the dissemination of information.

Exactly what is paper? It is a mass of cellulose fibers that are bonded together to create a diverse range of textures. Cotton, which has the longest and strongest fibers, is the most suitable material from which to produce paper.

There is something magical and unique, however, about handmade paper, particularly that which you produce yourself. Its aesthetic qualities are beyond dispute. This book will take you step by step through the process of making paper from both recycled paper and plant fibers. Making your own paper is inexpensive and at the same time environmentally friendly. Once you have mastered the technique of producing uniform sheets of recycled paper that may be used for cards, stationery, boxes, and books, you may want to move on to the slightly more involved process of making paper from plant fiber. Before you rush into paper made wholly from plant fiber, however, you might like to try introducing a handful of plant fiber to your vat of recycled pulp.

star book This tiny concertina book is made using an ingenious method of folding.

A brief history of paper

The development of paper, as we know it, began in China. A paper made from silk was available in that country; the first recorded use of it was in A.D. 105, and the process of making it was a closely guarded secret. Around A.D. 600, the process reached Korea, then Japan, before spreading to Samarkand in the eighth century. In 751, Samarkand fell to the Arabs and the secret of papermaking was taken back to North Africa. From North Africa the process was taken to Spain, and the Moors established the first paper mill on the Iberian Peninsula in about A.D. 1100, at the town of Xativa, in Spain.

The date and means of the introduction of papermaking into the rest of Europe is the subject of some dispute, but there is a reasonably well-documented claim that it came via the Arabs in North Africa, who had established trade routes with Amalfi, in Italy. From Italy, papermaking quickly spread to France, where a paper mill was established at Troyes. The craft finally reached England, briefly but successfully, in 1490 when John Tate, a mercer, began operating a mill at Hertford. However, it was not until 1589, when John Spilman, a goldsmith to Queen Elizabeth I, was granted Letters Patent for the exclusive right to make paper, that a successful paper mill, staffed by German workers, was established at Dartford, Kent.

All European paper before the eighteenth century was handmade, although the exact composition is still a mystery. Studies suggest that early paper was made from hemp or linen or a combination of both, in particular old rags and cordage. These were sorted, then soaked for weeks to cleanse them of impurities, soften the fibers and leave them more receptive to beating. The production methods of paper are well documented and the methods that handmade papermakers use today to form, couch, and dry paper are basically the same as those used in the Middle Ages.

A note on paper sizes

All of the projects in this book are based on the international standard paper sizes that are used by all countries except the U.S., Canada, and a few other countries in the Americas. A table showing the standard and U.S. sizes in both metric and imperial measurements is given at right.

envelopes This range of envelopes is made from handmade and commercial papers.

Paper sizes

International standard paper sizes
A0: 841 x 1189 mm (33⅛ x 46¾ inches)
A1: 594 x 841 mm (23⅜ x 33⅛ inches)
A2: 420 x 594 mm (16½ x 23⅜ inches)
A3: 297 x 420 mm (11¾ x 16½ inches)
A4: 210 x 297 mm (8¼ x 11¾ inches)
A5: 148 x 210 mm (5¹³⁄₁₆ x 8¼ inches)

American paper sizes
Letter (U.S.): 215.9 x 279.4 mm (8½ x 11 inches)
Legal (U.S.): 215.9 x 355.6 mm (8½ x 14 inches)
Tabloid (U.S.): 279.4 x 431.8 mm (11 x 17 inches)

Basic requirements for handmade paper

The process of making paper by hand involves making a pulp of fibers by beating soaked recycled paper or cooked plant fiber in a kitchen blender. The pulp is mixed in a tub of water, called the vat, and strained with a wire-meshed frame—the mold. The pulp is restrained by a second frame, called the deckle, which is placed on top of the mold. This gives the outer border of the paper its name, the deckle edge. After straining, the wet pulp that has been trapped by the mold and deckle is laid down onto soft felt covered with cloth, in a process known as "couching," from the French word *coucher*, meaning "to lay down." A stack of wet sheets of paper, separated by cloths, is called a post. The texture of the cloth will be imprinted on the paper, so if you want a smooth paper, you will need to use a fine-textured cloth. Any texture or crinkles in the cloth will be transferred through several adjoining sheets in the post of wet papers when they are later pressed, so couching cloths should be crease-free and placed carefully on the wet sheets.

Although the aim is to make interesting papers, the process itself can be very enjoyable, working with basic materials and water. You do not have to be "artistic," as the process itself allows you to develop ideas as you go. Furthermore, if you are not satisfied with the results, you can re-use or scrap your base materials, as these have cost you little except your time. There are few hard and fast rules for papermaking, and you will find, as you become more practiced, that you can develop techniques that suit you best.

You do not need to purchase a lot of expensive equipment, and you can often improvise. If you do not have a mold and deckle, you can make these by using two wooden frames of the same size. Nylon or wire mesh must be stapled tightly across one frame, as sagging mesh makes it difficult to couch the wet sheet of paper. A vat can be made by lining a polystyrene vegetable box with plastic, or you can use a large plastic storage box. For pressing, you can purchase a screw press, or make do with the inexpensive but perfectly functional alternative of two boards held together with two or four G-clamps. If no G-clamps are available, the pressing boards can be weighed down by putting any very heavy object, such as a large bucket of water, on top of them. Don't be tempted to stand on the boards, as they may be slippery and you could fall. This method is not as effective as using a screw press or G-clamps, but it will suffice if there are no other options.

What can be recycled?

Beautiful papers can be made by recycling many types of paper; however, the quality of the finished paper will never be better than that of the original paper, so it is best to start with good-quality scrap paper. Newspaper contains a significant amount of acid, and is not made to be long lasting, so it should never be used in hand papermaking. Egg cartons are also unsuitable. Non-glossy brochures, photocopy and computer paper, envelopes, art papers, and acid-free mount board are suitable. Shredded office paper is fine, but you need to be sure that there is no glue, sticky paper, or clear envelope window material included in it. Sometimes packs of prepared pulp are available from art and craft stores.

Using printed paper will result in small flecks in the handmade paper, which can look effective, depending on the intended use of your paper. Colored paper will create colored paper, though the end color may not be quite as bright as the original. Papers with unstable colors that run when wet are not suitable to recycle, as they add more color to the water than the pulp, and can cause stains throughout the post of wet papers. Good-quality paper napkins and tissue paper usually have strong permanent dyes that can be mixed with other, stronger papers. Colors can be mixed in a blender for uniform color, or pulps of various colors can be mixed in the vat for a mottled effect. Of course, color can also be created by adding commercial paper or cotton dyes to the pulp.

A better quality paper will be obtained by recycling acid-free art paper, mount board or cotton linter. Cotton linters are preprocessed cotton paper sheets available from specialty art suppliers; they can be used on their own or included with recycled paper. Offcuts of mount board can often be obtained from framing stores. Pure cotton fabric, such as old bed sheets, can also be recycled to make paper, though the process of pulping these materials requires more sophisticated equipment than a kitchen blender.

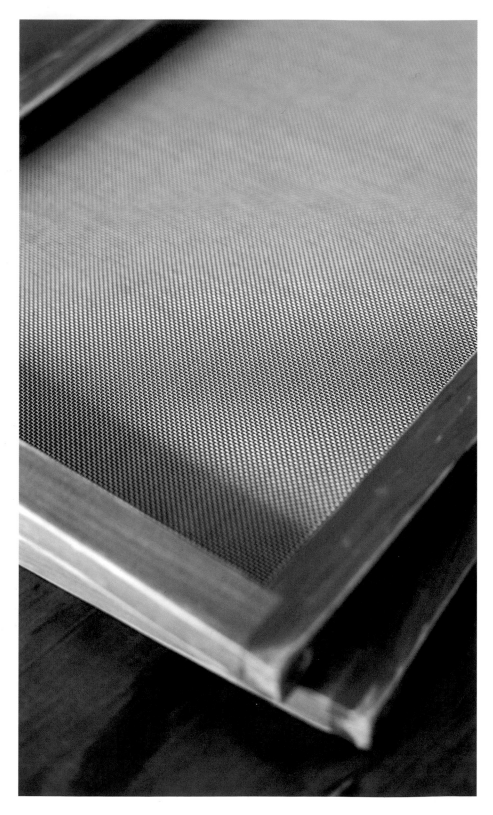

Equipment

The equipment that you need to start papermaking is simple and can be fairly easily improvised. Keen papermakers will buy better made and more sophisticated molds and deckles, perhaps in different shapes and sizes.

Mold and deckle A very basic mold and deckle can be made from two old same-sized picture frames and nylon screen mesh. If you are making your own mold and deckle in this way, note that the mesh must be very firmly stretched and stapled, as any sagging will cause the pulp to pool in the center. The best molds are made from high-grade stainless steel mesh (pictured left). A useful size for a mold is A4 or legal size; the resulting paper can be made smaller by cutting or tearing, if desired.

Envelope deckle (see page 31).

Tub or vat This should be at least 6 inches wider and longer than the outer edge of the deckle, and 10 inches or more deep.

Couching cloths These can be cotton, polycotton or nylon, such as diaper liners or kitchen wipes. To produce legal-size sheets, they will need to measure about 16 x 12 inches.

Two pieces of felt pad or sponge (such as carpet underlay) or thick papermaking felt, about 16 x 12 inches, for couching.

opposite A mold with good-quality stainless-steel mesh gives the best results.

right Any deep container large enough to accommodate the mold and deckle is suitable to use as a vat. A fine mesh strainer is also needed.

Kitchen blender (not a food processor). A secondhand store may provide this if you don't already have one.

Press For a simple press, use two wooden boards made of sealed plywood, 16 x 12 x ¾ inches, and two or four G-clamps. For best results, a G-clamp for each edge of the pressing board "sandwich" can be used.

Screw press This desirable luxury provides evenly distributed pressing across the post of wet sheets. A screw press still requires two pressing boards, as described above.

Drying boards Any flat, smooth surface such as a window or laminated work surface is suitable.

Paint roller

Buckets

Sponges or old towel.

Sieve One with a fine wire mesh is preferable. A colander is not suitable as the holes are too big and will allow the paper pulp to drain away as well as the water. Pulp can also be drained through a polyester organza bag with overlocked edges, placed inside a bucket with drainage holes drilled in the bottom.

Making recycled paper

There are six basic stages in making recycled paper:

1 Soaking Soaking torn-up pieces of paper.

2 Beating Processing the paper in a blender to make pulp, and adding to a vat of water.

3 Sheet formation Drawing a mold and deckle through the vat of pulp (also known as "pulling"), then allowing excess water to drain away.

4 Couching Laying the mold face down on top of a prepared surface and removing it to leave a sheet of paper behind.

5 Pressing A stack (or post) of wet sheets of paper is pressed between two boards using G-clamps, a heavy weight or a screw press. Ten or more sheets, depending on their thickness, can be pressed at the same time.

6 Drying The sheets can be dried flat on a board, or pegged to a line while still attached to their couching sheets.

Steps in making recycled paper

1 Tear or cut paper into small pieces, about 1 inch square, and soak in water overnight (or for about half an hour in hot water).

2 To make the pulp, add a small handful of soaked paper to the blender and top up with water to about three-quarters full. Do not overfill. Blend until the paper is mulched to look like porridge (20–30 seconds). No pieces of paper should be visible. Don't overload the blender, as too much paper will strain the motor. Transfer the beaten pulp to a clean bucket and repeat the blending process until all of the paper has been pulped.

3 Transfer some pulp to the vat and add water. Keep some pulp in the bucket to top up the vat and maintain the consistency of the pulp. The vat needs a sufficient depth of pulp and water to enable the mold and deckle to be drawn through it and brought out in a horizontal position without too much hesitation. You will need to experiment with the consistency of the pulp to obtain the thickness of the paper you require. The ratio of pulp to water determines the thickness: to test this, you need to pull the mold and deckle through the vat. For a thick sheet, the wet pulp can be ¼–⅜ inch thick; for a thinner sheet, you only need ⅛ inch of pulp on the mesh. Once the vat is "charged" to the desired consistency, you will only need to add an extra cupful of pulp after every two or three sheets of paper. Before making each sheet, stir the vat well to distribute the pulp evenly. Prepare a couching surface (see right).

Hints

If you damage the wet sheet or are dissatisfied with it before couching, do not scrape it off the mold. Simply turn the mold upsidedown and lay it against the surface of the water in the vat. The pulp will float off into the vat and can be stirred back in before forming a new sheet. Similarly, a couched sheet can be removed by carefully lifting the cloth, turning it over and floating the sheet back into the vat.

To prepare a couching surface, wet a piece of felt and place it onto one of the pressing boards. Cover with a couching cloth and wet thoroughly with clean water.

step one Tear or cut paper into small pieces and soak in water.

step two Place a small handful of paper in a blender and fill it three-quarters full with water.

step three Add the beaten paper pulp to the vat, adding water as desired.

Hints

If you have problems getting sheets to separate from the mold onto the couching cloth, you can gently press against the wire mesh with the palm of your hand or a sponge as you couch the paper. This can also help if you find that air bubbles are forming as you couch. Air bubbles may also form if the wire mesh is not taut. This can be counteracted by building up a pad in the center underneath the base felt, using a smaller piece of felt or folded newspaper.

Bubbles also sometimes occur when the mold is lifted off. Make sure you don't lift the mold straight up vertically. You may persuade air bubbles over to the edges of the sheet by re-lowering the screen and sponging down across it. Note, however, that when the sheet is pressed and dry, bubbles are rarely noticeable unless the paper is held up to the light.

4 Place the deckle on top of the mold with the mesh side against the deckle (see photograph below). Dip the mold and deckle into the vat at an angle of about 45 degrees, holding the two pieces firmly together with both hands, taking care that your fingers are not resting against the wire mesh. It is important to be relaxed, holding the mold firmly but not rigidly. Slide the mold and deckle completely under the surface of the water, then bring it to a horizontal position to scoop up the pulp, bending your elbows as you do so. Make sure you keep the mold and deckle level as you pull it out of the water, giving it a short, gentle shake from side to side before the water has all drained.

5 Either resting the mold on the table or holding it firmly in one hand, lift the deckle away with the other hand, taking care not to let drips fall on the newly formed paper sheet. Rest one edge of the mold along one side of the prepared couching cloth, laid out on top of a pressing board and felt pad with the exposed wet paper facing down toward the cloth. It will not fall off the mold. Steady the mold with one hand on the bottom edge, nearest the couching cloth.

6 Gently lay the wet paper flat against the couching cloth with a rolling motion, as if closing a book. Applying some pressure to the frame, follow through the action of the rolling, lifting the mold away from the paper in the process. The paper should stay on the couching cloth. Sometimes the first sheet may be difficult to couch if it is thin, so it best to make the first sheet thicker, and continue with thinner ones afterwards if you wish. (See Hints, left.)

step four Holding the mold and deckle firmly, draw it through the pulp in the vat.

step five Steady the mold with one hand on the bottom, nearest the couching cloth.

step six Roll the paper onto the couching cloth, as if closing a book.

7 Carefully place another couching cloth over the newly formed sheet. This cloth will quickly soak up water from the first sheet, but do not rub it or press hard on it as you may spoil the paper beneath. Make another sheet of paper in the same way, rolling it out on top of the first sheet. It is important to line it up to lie exactly on top of the first sheet: you may be able to make a post of ten or more papers. When the post is finished, cover the top sheet with another couching cloth, the second felt pad, and the second pressing board. Put the resulting sandwich in a screw press or attach G-clamps and tighten securely. You will be surprised at how much water flows out, and you can facilitate the draining process by standing the pressing boards at an angle. Pressing not only removes the water, but also makes the paper stronger by forcing the fibers together. Leave the post pressing for at least an hour, or overnight if you wish.

8 The simplest method of drying the pressed paper is to carefully lift each sheet of paper while still attached to the couching cloth, peg it onto a clothesline and leave to dry (paper dried by this method is more likely to cockle, or buckle). Alternatively, lay the paper against a smooth surface, such as a glass window or laminated work surface, and roll a paint roller evenly over the couching cloth to ensure the paper underneath is adhering to the surface. Roll the paper again to firm down the edges and remove any air bubbles. Rolling onto glass or other smooth surfaces will produce a very smooth paper.

9 When the paper is completely dry, remove it from the drying surface. It can be pressed again between dry boards if desired.

step seven Use G-clamps or a screw press to press the post and remove water.

step eight Use a paint roller to roll the pressed sheets onto a flat drying surface.

step nine Remove the couching cloth from the dry paper, not the paper from the cloth.

Inclusions and variations

An endless variety of beautiful papers can be created by adding different inclusions to a vat of white or colored recycled pulp, then forming the sheets in the usual way. These inclusions can be plant material, colored papers or even tea leaves. Metallic papers may be cut up small and included. Any non-cellulose material needs to be very small and fine to mesh with the paper and not ruin the blender. Multicolored sewing threads can be cut into small pieces (they are apt to tangle and form lumps if they are too lengthy). If using cotton or silk thread or wool, separate the fibers using a pin, then cut into short pieces and put into the blender. These will appear as very fine hairs in the paper.

The simplest way to create a decorative effect with recycled paper is to add an extra cupful of roughly or regularly beaten pulp of a different color to the vat of pulp. Stir it through gently. Some of the colors will blend, but some will stay separate. This may not be very obvious when the pulp is wet, but when the paper dries, flecks of color will be easily seen, and beautiful multicolored papers can be made in this way.

Finely shredded paper, confetti, or small pieces of colored paper can also be added. Scraps with interesting words, snippets of text or foreign scripts are very effective. Some will be completely buried, some will float at random on the surface: sometimes what appears on the underneath is more interesting than what you can see on the top. Test to ensure that the paper you are adding is a stable color, as some papers have unstable dyes and the color may run when wet, creating effects you don't want. Metallic or plastic scraps are difficult to embed in the pulp, and may fall off the dry paper, so if you want to try anything like tinsel, you will have more success with small pieces.

Dried pressed flowers and plant fibers look beautiful in paper. Small flowers, such as cornflowers, hydrangeas (shown at right), geraniums, and bougainvilleas, or small pressed maple leaves are a few suggestions, but many others are suitable. Some flowers will "bleed" color (usually brown) into the surrounding paper and the sheets underneath, so it is a good idea to do a test run first. Colored petals and pressed flowers may be cooked before inclusion to prevent bleeding. The same applies to some leaves. You can also use dried grasses or pieces of thin, soft bark to create an interest. If you are adding anything that is thick, you will need to have enough pulp to make a thick sheet of paper to accommodate it. Don't use anything that is stiff, as this may pop out of the dry paper or tear it.

Start by adding small amounts of inclusions to the vat, and build up slowly; it is much easier to add more than to extract excess from the vat. You can combine different varieties, such as plant fibers and shredded paper, but don't overdo it.

Color

If using dyes to color paper, follow the instructions on the bottle and wear gloves. One of the simplest methods to obtain color is to begin with colored papers as the original material to recycle: colors may be mixed in the blender, much as you would mix paint together to get the desired shade. The paper will dry several shades lighter than it appears when wet, so make the pulp darker than the finished color you are striving for. (Pinch a small piece of the pulp firmly between thumb and forefinger to get an idea of how it will look when dry.) It is also possible to add several different colored batches of pulp into the one vat without first blending them together. This will give the paper a more "tweedy" effect.

There are many other ways in which a huge range and variety of papers may be made, and these will be dealt with in the following pages of this book. Techniques include producing colored papers; adding inclusions as explained opposite; laminating, which in its most basic form is laying and drying two sheets together; embedding, showing ways in which decorative elements can be deliberately placed and anchored on the sheet or can be captured between two sheets of paper; and embossing, where low-relief or three-dimensional objects can leave their impressions in the paper.

Making paper from plant fiber

The process of forming a sheet of paper from plant fiber is much the same as that used to make a sheet of paper from recycled paper or cotton linter. Much more time is involved, however, in harvesting, cutting up, cooking, rinsing, and beating the pulp before it can be formed into a sheet of paper, which may or may not require the inclusion of a formation aid to help suspend the fibers in the water, and to slow down drainage to enable the formation of an even sheet.

The variety of papers that can be made from plant fiber is virtually limitless, ranging from coarse opaque papers to delicate, translucent, almost gossamerlike paper. The paper can be very uniform or homogenous, or much more fibrous with wispy edges, depending on how long the pulp is blended and whether or not a deckle is used. The range of colors is extensive, from off-white to cream, through every hue of brown and green and sometimes surprising and unusual colors. Different parts of a plant (such as leaves and stems) can also give quite different colors. While the plant itself determines the color of the paper (for example, banana leaves or stem are always brown, pampas grass leaves are always green), the time of year of harvesting may also cause variations in color. So, also, can the method of storage (such as decomposing in a plastic bag versus being cooked immediately after picking). Plant fiber paper is full of surprises.

Many plant fibers can be turned into paper but some are much better than others. In Japan, "kozo"—the inner bark of the Japanese paper mulberry tree—is a preferred fiber, and two of the most successful fibers in Australia are from the banana tree and the New Zealand flax (*Phormium tenax*). Wherever you live there are plants, including even vegetables, that are suitable for making interesting papers. You might try corn husks or globe artichoke leaves, the main consideration being the presence of a high cellulose-fiber content.

Plants useful for papermaking fall, in general, into three broad categories:
- Grasses (such as rushes, reeds, sedges, papyrus, bamboo).
- Bast fibers and stem fibers (such as stems of ginger lily, strelitzia, canna lily, agapanthus, kangaroo paw, banana, nettles, clover). The bast is the inner bark of woody stems or trunks such as paper mulberry, daphne, and hibiscus.
- Bladelike leaves (such as gladiolus, iris, red-hot poker, agapanthus, pineapple, and yucca).

In general it is the monocotyledons, which have parallel veins, that are most productive of the cellulose fibers needed for paper.

Equipment

Same equipment as used for recycled paper (page 10), plus:

Secateurs to harvest plants

Gardening gloves to protect hands

Large enamel or stainless steel boiler to cook fiber (it takes a large amount of plant fiber to yield quite a small amount of cellulose fiber)

Alkali such as caustic soda, soda ash (sodium carbonate), or washing soda to break down fiber in cooking

Formation aid: natural, such as the liquid made by soaking okra or prickly pear in water, or synthetic, available from specialist papermaking suppliers

Wooden stick for stirring

Tongs for removing bag of fiber after cooking—or you can use the stirring stick to lift it out

Nylon or net drawstring bag (pillowcase size) to hold fiber during cooking and rinsing

Rubber gloves to protect hands from caustic soda—it is particularly dangerous for eyes

Protective glasses (when using caustic)

Hose and access to an outdoor source of water

Plant material to be cooked

pH testing strips

Steps for making paper from plant fiber

If you are not ready to use harvested plant material immediately, seal it in a strong plastic bag where it may be left for long periods. This process is called "retting": bacterial decay starts to break down the plants and make the cooking process faster.

You can try cooking some softer plants without caustic soda; for example, the green tops of leeks will fall apart after about half an hour of cooking and although they contain a lot of other material besides cellulose fiber, a brittle, attractive, but not very strong paper can be made with just a quick whiz of the blender. (Leek is also an attractive additive to recycled paper. The smell will soon disappear after the paper is dried.) With plant-fiber paper, there is nothing like experimenting to see what you can get, and what you are capable of.

Rinsed fibers should be pH neutral (you can test them with a pH strip: 7 is neutral). A little vinegar may be added to neutralize the alkali, but beware: acid is detrimental to the archival quality of the paper. Dilute any alkaline liquid that remains in the boiler and dispose of it down the drain.

1 Harvest the plant material. Some long stems may benefit by being split lengthwise, or pounded with a mallet before cutting. When ready to cook, rinse off any dirt or sand, cut the plant into 1–2 inch lengths and place in a nylon bag. If the bag doesn't have a drawstring, tie a knot in the top or tie with a piece of nylon (not cotton or jute) string for ease of removal.

2 Cook in a stainless steel, enamel, or copper container (preferably outdoors or in a well-ventilated room) in an alkaline solution of caustic soda, soda ash (sodium carbonate), or washing soda. If using caustic soda (which is the fastest method, but must be used with caution) the ratio is 15–20 percent of the dry weight of the fiber—roughly 3 teaspoons of caustic to 12 cups of cold water. *For safety, add the caustic to the cold water, not the water to the caustic. Also, always use cold water, never warm, hot, or boiling.* If you want to avoid using caustic soda you can use soda ash (sodium carbonate) or washing soda in the proportion of 9 ounces of dry plant material to 8 teaspoons soda ash or washing soda diluted in 12 cups of cold water, but it will take longer to break down the plant fiber. The precise quantities will be determined by the physical bulk of the plant fiber to be cooked; it should be covered by the water. Bring the water to the boil and stir the fiber occasionally. Avoid at all times breathing in the fumes and, if indoors, switch on the exhaust fan. If you have a hotplate that can be used in the open air this is better, as the smell can be quite potent.

step one Harvest plant material and cut it into small pieces for cooking.

step two Place plant material in a nylon bag and boil in an alkaline solution.

3 The plant material is cooked when the fibers separate easily: using a gloved hand, rub them between thumb and forefinger, or push a small quantity against the side of the boiler with the stirring stick. Cooking times can vary from one hour to as much as six hours for very tough plants. (The four variables—quantity of plant fiber, volume of water, strength of alkali and the toughness of the plant fiber—will all interact to determine the cooking time.) When cooked, leave the fiber in the boiler to cool, then remove the bag with tongs or a wooden stick and run water from a garden hose through it to rinse it very thoroughly, shaking or stirring the fiber. It may be best to soak it in a vat or bucket to ensure all the caustic soda is removed. The water should run clear. This is the point at which a pH strip is useful to test that the acid/alkali balance is neutral.

4 When the fiber is fully rinsed, it may be beaten. It may need to be cut into smaller pieces or beaten with a wooden mallet before being put in the blender. Don't put too much into the blender at once. If the fiber tangles around the blade, it needs to be cut shorter. Fibers can be blended very finely to give a homogenous sheet of paper, but often there is more character and texture in the paper if some fibers are less well blended. Place the processed fiber in a vat and proceed with forming, couching, pressing, and drying as for recycled paper (see pages 13–15). If the water drains too quickly through the fiber to allow the formation of an even sheet of paper, add formation aid; a rough guide is a couple of cupfuls (about 17 fl oz) to a vat of pulp, stirring well with the hand. You will notice a little resistance in the water and it will become less splashy.

Formation aid

Natural formation aid can be obtained from okra (*Abelmoschus esculentus*, a vegetable) or prickly pear (various species of *Opuntia*, a type of cactus). Okra is in season in spring, but it can be frozen for later use. Cut four or five pods of okra or lobes of prickly pear into chunks, enclose in a net bag to stop seeds escaping, and place in a bucket of water overnight. Both okra and prickly pear give off a slimy substance (known as mucilage) that can be added slowly to the vat to assist the formation of the sheets of paper. Strain before use.

Synthetic formation aid can be purchased in powder form at papermaking suppliers. It should be prepared eight hours before it is required. A teaspoon of the powder is mixed with denatured alcohol, and then added to 4 cups of water in a blender and processed for 45 seconds. It can then be strained through cheesecloth in a sieve to eradicate any fine lumps, which can cause "fish eyes" (small circular blemishes) in the paper. It can be stored in the refrigerator.

step three Once plant material is cooked and rinsed, it should be pH neutral.

step four Beat cooked fibers in a blender until you achieve the desired consistency.

Thick plant fiber paper

1 Chop plant fiber into small pieces and blend, so that some is well blended and some still retains its fibrous quality. Add 2 cups of formation aid to the vat, stirring around well, and pull sheets as for recycled paper. (Formation aid assists the suspension of fibers in the water, and also slows drainage through the mold to allow fibers to be spread more evenly). Make sure that any wispy fibers overhanging the deckle are flicked back onto the wet sheet, or they may damage the sheet when the deckle is lifted.

2 Remove the deckle carefully to avoid pulling any of the paper off the mold. Couch, press, and roll out to dry.

3 Mix other cooked plant fibers into the vat—some may be chopped into the vat without blending to add to the textural interest of the paper. The addition of white or colored recycled pulp can make lovely paper.

step one Flick long fibers that hang over the edge of the deckle back on the mold

step two Carefully remove the deckle, then couch, press, and dry the sheet.

step three The use of different plant fibers gives varied color and texture.

Transparent plant fiber paper

1 Using a thinner concentration of pulp (and adding formation aid), do a shallow scoop without using the deckle. This will allow a thinner coating of fiber on the mold, and also give wispy edges. It can be couched and rolled out to dry as usual.

2 As some fine pulps are a little more difficult to couch than thicker pulps, a small screen with stretched nylon may be made for the purpose. Or a piece of nylon may be stretched over the mold before dipping and the pulp may be dried directly on this without the need for couching or rolling onto a drying surface.

3 When the sheet of paper is completely dry, peel off carefully. (It is often surprising how strong the thin plant fiber paper can be.) Alternatively, hang the sheet (still on its couching cloth) on a clothesline to dry.

step one Use the mold without the deckle to allow a thinner coverage of fibers.

step two If using stretched nylon over the mold, you can let the paper dry without couching.

step three Alternatively, hang the couched paper on a clothesline to dry.

Laminating

Laminating is the process of laying two sheets together without a separating cloth. They then meld to form a single sheet. This technique has many variations, the simplest being a plain sheet with a different color on each side. It is also the basic technique used in some of the more complex projects in this book, such as embedding (see page 26).

In the example on these pages, laminating is used to create the illusion of embedded dried leaves in a sheet of paper. This technique gives the appearance of embedded leaves without the brittle nature of such inclusions undermining the paper's structure. The process involves using plastic templates on the mold to create voids in the first sheet of paper. A second, solid sheet of a darker color is pulled and couched directly on top of the first sheet. When the resulting layers are pressed, rolled, and dried together, a single sheet of paper is the result.

step one Cut design elements from a plastic sheet such as an overhead transparency.

step two The shapes will adhere to the mold when wet.

step three Carefully remove the plastic templates before couching the sheet.

1 Draw or trace the elements of your design on paper. Lay a clear plastic sheet (such as an overhead transparency) over the paper, trace the shapes onto it, then cut them out.

2 Arrange them as desired on the mold. When wet, the plastic shapes will adhere to the mold and deckle as placed, and pulp will be dispersed away from the plastic parts of the design when you pull the sheet.

3 Once the water has drained, carefully remove the plastic shapes (use a needle to lift the edges) before couching.

4 Pull a sheet of a second color, which will show through the spaces in the first sheet. Couch this sheet directly on top of the first layer of pulp with no separating cloth. Make sure to align the sheets perfectly.

5 Press together: all the fibers will meld to form one sheet.

6 Dry the pressed sheets on the couching cloth or roll them onto a smooth drying surface.

step four Couch a second sheet directly on top of the first one.

step five Press the couched sheets together to form one sheet.

step six Dry the paper on the couching cloth or on a smooth surface, then carefully peel it off.

Embedding

Embedding is a process that uses the basic technique of laminating as described in the last project; however, it puts "filling" (an object or image) in the sandwich created by couching two layers, or partial layers, of pulp together. Sometimes the top layer of pulp will be semitransparent plant fiber, or the object or image will be revealed by pulling some of the second layer of pulp away. Alternatively, it is possible to dip the mold only partially in the pulp and thus only partially trap the object or image between the two layers of pulp, as in the example on this page.

1 Couch a base sheet and lay on it the material to be embedded, such as dried and pressed plants.

2 Cover the material to be embedded with another sheet. In this case, just a partial dip of the mold into the vat has created a narrow strip of translucent paper.

3 Press and roll out onto a drying board, front side uppermost (this will mean turning the post over and removing the bottom cloth in order to roll it out).

step one Lay the material to be embedded on the couched paper.

step two Pull a second, partial sheet of translucent plant fibers without using a deckle.

step three The pressed fibers trap the embedded material between the layers.

Embossing

Paper pulp will faithfully take on the contours of any surface on which it is laid, and this leads to a world of exciting experimentation with embossing. The process described below uses the pressing process to help emboss the image, so only low-relief, unbreakable material should be used.

1 Lay out a pressing board, sponge, and a wet couching cloth to receive the sheet of pulp (which should not be too thin, or it may tear). Place the material to be embossed onto the pulp and cover with another nylon couching cloth and pressing board. Press as before.

2 Remove the paper from the press and, turning the "sandwich" over, remove the bottom cloth. Carefully place the sheet on the drying board. With the top cloth still covering the sheet, roll very firmly with a paint roller to get the maximum definition in the embossing.

3 Alternatively, use an absorbent sponge to enhance the embossed impression. Allow the sheet to dry completely before removing the embossing material.

step one Place the material to be embossed on top of the couched sheet.

step two After pressing, remove the bottom couching cloth only and roll firmly.

step three Pressing with an absorbent sponge will give greater definition to the embossing.

Projects using handmade paper

Once you have made your own paper, what do you do with it? The following projects give ideas for different uses for handmade paper or for commercial papers: envelopes, cards, and different types of handmade books (concertina books, folded books, simple sewn books with various types of covers and bindings), stationery folders, and even framed artworks. The projects here give just a taste of the uses to which beautiful papers can be put.

Equipment

The following equipment and tools are referred to in the projects.

Awl A pointed metal spike for making fine, barely visible holes in paper. Usually an awl needs only hand pressure. A pin or needle inserted into the end of a round craft-knife handle can also be used.

Bone folder This is the bookbinder's most useful tool. It is used for scoring, folding, and creasing paper, smoothing pasted surfaces, and turning edges of paper over cover boards. The bone folder is flat with blunt edges, rounded at one end and pointed at the other. It is usually made of whalebone. A 4–6 inch bone folder is suitable.

Brushes Various sizes are used, depending on the need. Brushes range from stiff flat ones for pasting to large round ones for general gluing purposes.

Cutting mat A 12 x 18-inch self-healing cutting mat is a good size.

Dividers These can be used for all kinds of measuring and marking.

Hole punch For making neat, round holes in paper or board. Use with a hammer, if necessary, to cut through board.

Knife A scalpel with replaceable blade or a retractable craft knife can be used for cutting paper, card stock, and board.

Metal ruler The ruler should be at least 12 inches long. A layer of masking tape attached to the back will help to prevent it from slipping.

Needles Regular bookbinding needles have a slightly blunt point with a head about the same thickness as the body of the needle to avoid increasing the size of the hole when sewing sections. A tapestry needle or darning needle with a small eye is a suitable alternative.

Pencil and eraser Ensure the pencil is sharp when marking cutting lines—avoid thick lines, which may vary your measurements. A black (B) pencil is suitable.

Pressing boards These are used in place of a screw press. They can be screwed down with G-clamps; alternatively, cover two or three bricks with paper and place on top of the boards to press books. Small lead weights are also useful for small books.

Set square An L-shaped measuring device, preferably of steel, which is used for measuring and for obtaining square corners and right angles.

Making envelopes

If you plan to use your handmade paper for cards, notes, or letters, creating matching envelopes will be high on your list of extra skills to acquire.

Envelope deckles create paper ready to fold into envelope shapes.

Using an envelope deckle

1 Handmade envelopes are made in the same way as sheets of paper, using an envelope deckle. If you can't acquire an envelope deckle from a supplier, you can easily make one from ⅛-inch foam core, sealed plywood, cardboard, or linoleum. The outer dimensions of the envelope deckle should be the same as the mold. Cut the envelope shape from the middle of the board (use Templates A and E, pages 33 and 35, or use an opened-out envelope as a template). The outer area of the board will be your envelope deckle. Coat the envelope deckle with several layers of shellac or marine varnish to ensure it is waterproof.

2 Instead of making an envelope deckle, you could use the center of the deckle board as a template to trace and cut the shape from a legal-size sheet of handmade paper. A common envelope size for handmade stationery is 4½ x 6½ inches.

3 Position the envelope deckle between your mold and paper deckle to secure it, then proceed to make the envelopes in the same way as you make a sheet of paper. Paper for envelopes should be of medium weight. The envelopes can, however, be lined with other handmade papers or decorative commercial papers.

4 To fold the envelope, turn in the sides first. Turn up the bottom flap and glue to the sides.

5 Double-sided tape is ideal to use to seal the envelope, especially if you are making gift stationery.

Hint

Before folding envelopes, it is helpful to make a cardboard template of the same size that you require for the finished envelope. Place the template in position on the paper and turn up the sides of the envelope all round. This way you will ensure that all your envelopes are a uniform size. This is particularly important when making packs of handmade stationery.

Japanese origami-style envelope

Use Template B1, page 35

Fold along the fold lines starting with the top left-hand corner of the page and then the bottom right-hand corner. The edges of the folded paper will meet in the middle. Then fold along the fold lines from the bottom left-hand corner and then from the top right-hand corner. A small triangle of paper will protrude over the edge of the envelope. This triangle should be folded over the edge and can be sealed with a decorative seal as part of the back of the envelope, or with a postage stamp as part of the front of the envelope. By adjusting the dimensions you can make the envelope smaller or larger. There is no need to glue this envelope. It can also work as a letter that is folded to form its own envelope.

Variation of origami-style envelope

Use Template B2, page 33

Fold from corner A along fold line. Then fold from corner B along fold line. Fold down from corner C along fold line. These three folds will meet (see diagram 1A).

Measure 3⅞ inches from the top of the fold line formed when corner C was folded down. Fold backwards. Measure 3⅞ inches from the top of the fold line just formed and then fold over again. Tuck corner D into the triangular section on the bottom left (see diagram 1B). This creates a small folder with a number of pockets in which to display photos or other items. Diagram 1C shows the back of the finished envelope.

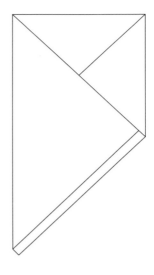

diagram 1A
Variation of origami-style envelope; folded so that the first three folds meet

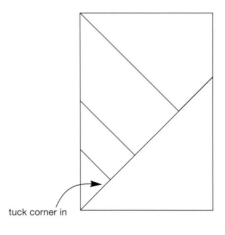

diagram 1B
Finished view of front of variation of origami-style envelope

tuck corner in

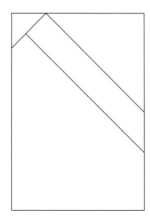

diagram 1C
Finished view of back of variation of origami-style envelope

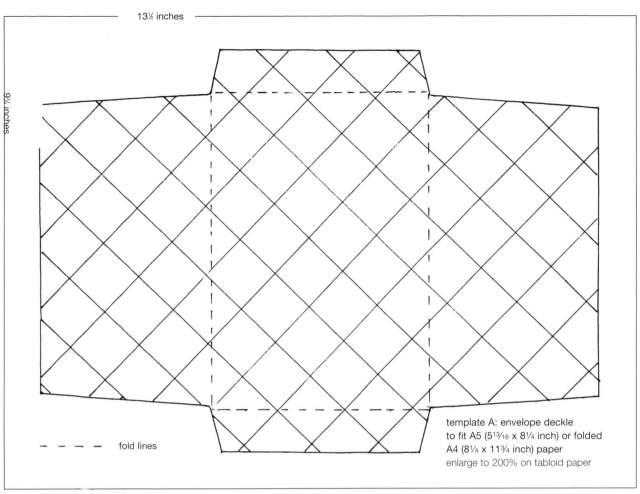

13½ inches

9¾ inches

– – – – fold lines

template A: envelope deckle
to fit A5 (5¹³⁄₁₆ x 8¼ inch) or folded
A4 (8¼ x 11¾ inch) paper
enlarge to 200% on tabloid paper

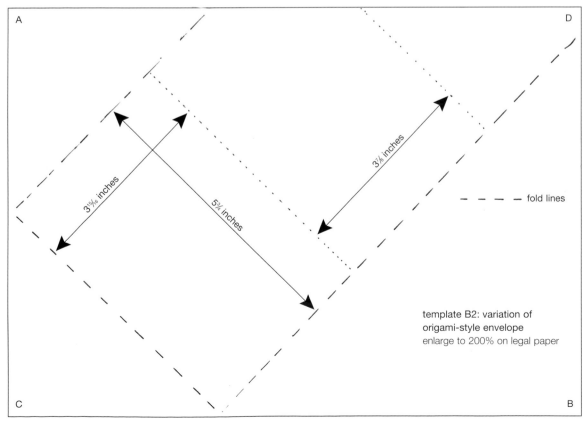

A

D

3¹⁵⁄₁₆ inches

5¼ inches

3⅞ inches

– – – – fold lines

template B2: variation of
origami-style envelope
enlarge to 200% on legal paper

C

B

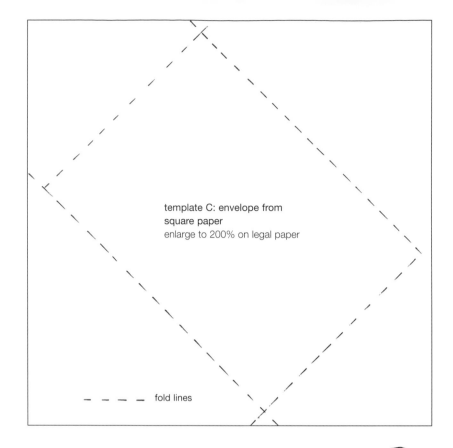

template C: envelope from
square paper
enlarge to 200% on legal paper

— — — fold lines

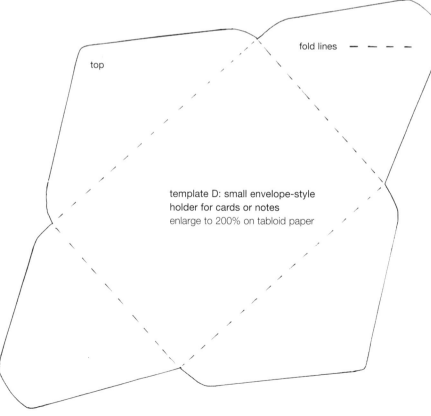

fold lines — — — —

top

template D: small envelope-style
holder for cards or notes
enlarge to 200% on tabloid paper

Envelope from
square paper

Use Template C, left
Score on the fold lines. Fold in the sides
first, then the bottom. Apply glue to the
edges of the bottom section of the envelope
to secure it in place. Lining paper can be
added before you fold, and decorative
scissors can be used to give an interesting
edge to the flap of the envelope and the
lining paper.

Small envelope-style
holder for cards or notes

Use Template D, left
Make a template from a piece of acetate to
keep for future use. Cut out the envelope,
score the lines, and fold over the sides first.
Glue the small overlap. Fold up the bottom
and glue along the edges to secure to the
sides. Use double-sided tape or a sticker to
close the envelope.

Gift-card envelope

Use Template F, page 35
This makes an envelope for a gift card
measuring approximately 2½ x 2¼ inches.
Cut out the envelope, score the lines, and
fold over the sides first. Fold up the bottom
and glue along the edges to secure to the
sides. Use double-sided tape or a sticker to
close the envelope.

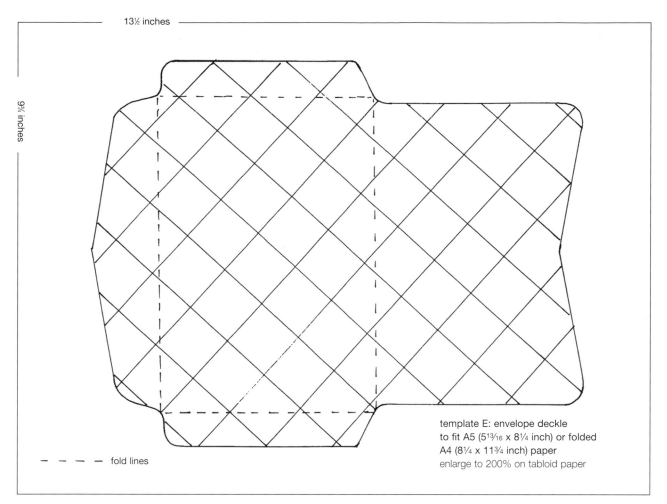

13½ inches

9¾ inches

template E: envelope deckle
to fit A5 (5¹³⁄₁₆ x 8¼ inch) or folded
A4 (8¼ x 11¾ inch) paper
enlarge to 200% on tabloid paper

- - - - - fold lines

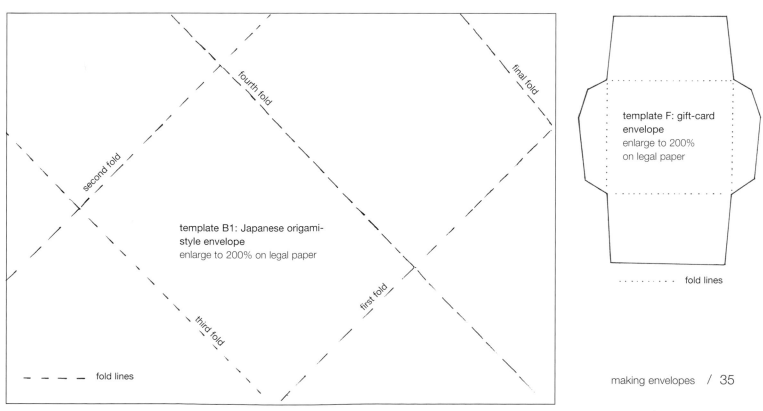

fourth fold

final fold

second fold

template B1: Japanese origami-
style envelope
enlarge to 200% on legal paper

third fold

first fold

- - - - - fold lines

template F: gift-card
envelope
enlarge to 200%
on legal paper

· · · · · · · · · fold lines

Trifold card

This simple card showcases your handmade paper, both in the card itself and in the collage of paper and inclusions that appears in the window. Careful measuring and cutting are required. Use thick, stiff paper or thin card stock, as you want the card to stand on its own.

step two Cut a window from the center panel using a craft knife and a guide if needed.

Materials

Legal-size sheet of
  handmade paper
Scrap card for window
  template
Small pieces of handmade
  paper, fabric, ribbon, fibers,
  charms, and other found
  objects for collage
Matching paper for envelope

Tools

Craft knife
Pencil
Ruler
Self-healing cutting mat
Bone folder
White school glue and brush
  for applying
Double-sided adhesive tape

1 On the back of sheet of paper about 8¼ x 11½ inches, mark the paper into thirds across its width. Score with a bone folder or the back of a knife and fold both end panels inward.

2 Open out the card, lay it on a self-healing cutting mat, and cut a window in the central panel to the required size: in the example pictured, the window measures 6 x 2⅜ inches. You may like to use a template cut from scrap card, as shown in the photograph. This allows you to be certain of the position of the window, before you cut the paper with a craft knife. Rescore the folds if necessary.

3 Build up a collage on the inside of the first flap (experiment with pieces of handmade paper, natural objects, fragments of writing, or anything you find pleasing). Test the composition with reference to the window before you glue it into place.

4 Adhere the two front panels of the card together with double-sided tape or white school glue that has been diluted a little.

5 To make an envelope, take a second sheet, lay the card diagonally across it, and fold up the sides around the card. Glue down two sides and the bottom fold to create an envelope (similar to Template B1, page 35).

Fan card

Clever folding makes this three-dimensional
card a striking yet simple project to demonstrate
the texture and color contrasts of your handmade
paper. Use a thick card stock for the base and
highlight the details with a translucent but
textured overlay.

This card can also be used as the cover of
a small booklet, as shown in the photograph
at right, by sewing additional folded pages
to the left or right fold of the middle section
instead of gluing in a single page. See the
section on simple sewn books (pages 85–87)
for instructions on pamphlet stitch.

Materials
heavyweight paper, 5 x 13½ inches, for card
medium-weight decorative paper, 4¼ inches
 square, to decorate front of card
medium-weight plain paper, 4¾ x 8¼ inches,
 to insert in card for message

Tools
Craft glue
Bone folder
Metal ruler

Create an artificial deckle on the edge of commercially manufactured paper.

Hint

To create an artificial deckle on commercially manufactured paper or card stock, rest the bottom of the paper or card on a work surface. Hold the top of the paper or card between the forefinger and thumb and tap firmly with the edge of a metal ruler (see above). This method will not work on thin paper, but is excellent for thick paper.

1 Score and fold the heavy paper into three sections measuring, from left, 4¼, 4¼ and 5 inches, as shown in Diagram 1 opposite.

2 Glue the decorative paper, which should complement the main card color, to the front of the section that measures 5 inches square. See Diagram 2.

3 Diagram 3 shows all fold lines. To construct the right-hand side of the fan, measure 1¼ inches from the top right-hand edge of the card, down the right-hand side of the decorated section. Make a light mark. Score a line with a bone folder from this mark to the bottom left-hand corner, as shown in Diagram 4.

4 Fold the front of the card on the score line, as shown in Diagram 4, and press down with the bone folder to make a crisp fold. Leave folded.

5 Place the ruler from the top right-hand corner to the bottom left-hand corner. Move the ruler back about ⅟₃₂ inch, and score a line between the bottom left corner and the top of the fan, as shown in Diagram 4.

6 Fold the card back so that the fold lies exactly on the diagonal between the top right and bottom left corners. This completes the right-hand side of the fan.

7 To construct the left-hand side of the fan, measure 1¼ inches along the top edge of the card from the right-hand corner. Make a light mark. Score a line from this mark to the bottom left corner. See Diagram 5.

8 Fold on the score line and rub down lightly with the bone folder. Open the card and turn it over so that you can work from the back of the fan.

9 Place a steel ruler on the diagonal between the top triangular section that is forming the point of the fan and the bottom right-hand corner. Move the ruler about $\frac{1}{32}$ inch to the left, to ensure that the score line is exactly on the diagonal, and score a line between the bottom right-hand corner and the top of the card.

10 Fold back on the score line and rub down with the bone folder. The two sides of the fan should lie together on the diagonal.

11 Fold the plain paper in half and apply a thin line of glue to the folded edge. Glue the folded edge to the left- or right-hand fold of the middle section of the card. The plain paper insert is to enable you to write a greeting or other message.

To vary the position of the fan, experiment with the dimensions for folding; that is, measure $1\frac{5}{8}$ inches from the top corner instead of $1\frac{1}{4}$ inches. Do this on scrap paper and keep practicing the variations until you are happy with the results.

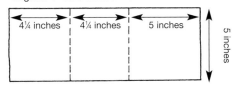

diagram 1 Card divided into three sections.

$4\frac{1}{4}$ inches $4\frac{1}{4}$ inches   5 inches   5 inches

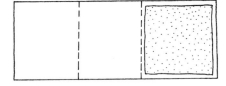

diagram 2 Contrasting paper glued to front.

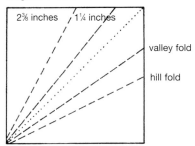

diagram 3 Fold lines

$2\frac{3}{8}$ inches $1\frac{1}{4}$ inches

valley fold

hill fold

diagram 4 Right-hand section

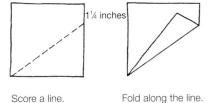

$1\frac{1}{4}$ inches

Score a line.   Fold along the line.   Score a line from bottom corner to top of fan.   Fold along the line.

diagram 5 Left-hand section

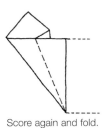

Score another line.   Fold on the line.   Score again and fold.

Stationery folder

Presentation is everything. When you have created handmade stationery—cards, note paper, and envelopes—you will want to make a sturdy and stylish folder to enclose your precious creations. A large sheet of paper can be folded and decorated to make a unique presentation folder, which you can give as a gift, or keep for yourself to preserve your work until you are ready to put it to use. This folder fits papers up to 6 x 8 inches in size. Decorate the folder with similar materials to those you have used on the enclosed stationery paper.

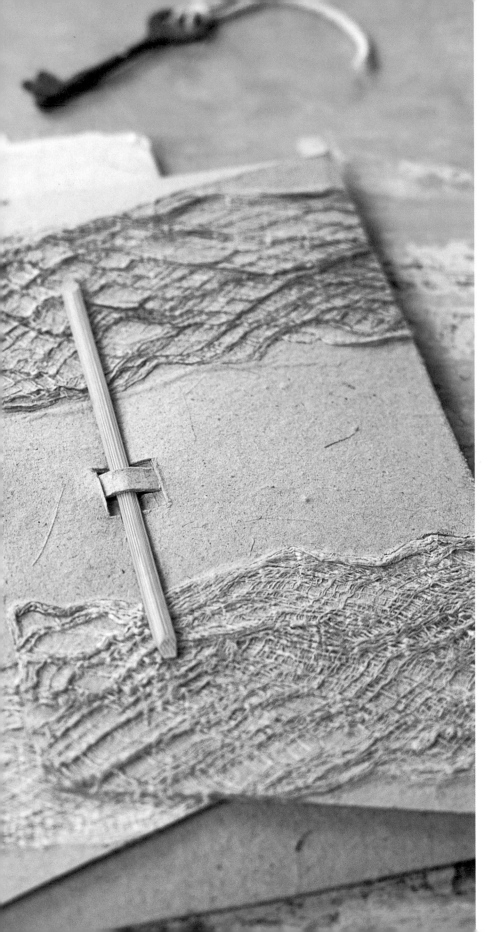

Materials

Sheet of handmade paper at least 15 x 10
  inches, decorated as desired, using
  laminating, embossing, or embedding
  techniques
Woven interfacing or diaper liner
Small flat stick

Tools

Craft knife
Metal ruler
Self-healing cutting mat
Glue
Bone folder

step two Cut out the shape of the stationery folder using a craft knife.

step three Glue a small piece of woven interfacing to reinforce the fastening.

1 First form a sheet of paper at least 15 x 10 inches, or use a commercial sheet of paper. When you are creating the paper, you may add a design feature to the right-hand external end of the paper by laminating, embedding, or embossing. Press, roll, and dry the sheet.

2 Using the template provided at right, a ruler, and a sharp craft knife, cut out the shape of the folder.

3 Glue a small piece of woven interfacing or diaper liner on the back of the top flap section where it will be cut for the fastening, and cut out a small square

opening as marked on the template. Cut two slots in the underflap, as indicated in the template, beginning the cuts 1 inch in from the edge of the folder.

4 Score along the fold lines, using a bone folder. Fold along the creases.

5 Fold along the scored lines and crease firmly with a bone folder.

6 Slide a flat stick under the strip to close the folder securely.

step four Use a bone folder to score the fold lines.

step five Crease firmly along the scored lines with a bone folder.

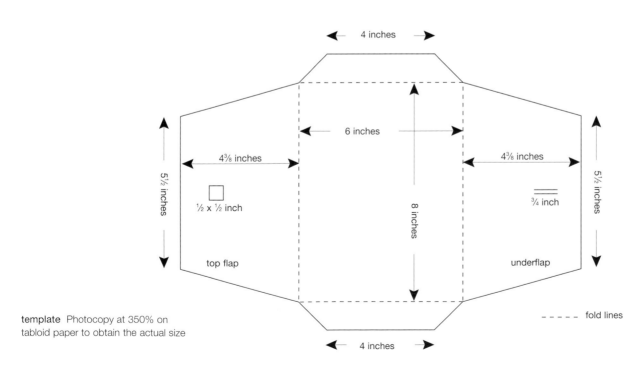

template Photocopy at 350% on tabloid paper to obtain the actual size

4 inches

6 inches

4⅜ inches

5½ inches

½ x ½ inch

top flap

4⅜ inches

¾ inch

5½ inches

8 inches

underflap

- - - - fold lines

4 inches

Laminated paper folder

This project uses the basic laminating process

to trap string between two layers of paper, thus

forming a basic binding. The resulting folder has

a loose structure, so the use of natural fibers and

textured paper adds to the rustic or primitive

appearance of the completed project.

Lengths of string are left protruding from the

open edges of the laminated sheets, thus

providing a means of fastening the folder.

Note that only natural cellulose fibers (such as

cotton, string, linen, jute, hemp, and ramie) will

bond with the paper; ribbons or yarns made

from other fibers are not suitable.

Materials
Paper pulp and water
String or fine rope, of a natural cellulose fiber

Tools
Vat
Mold and deckle
Pressing boards
Felt pads
Couching cloths
G-clamps

step one The pressing apparatus must be a little larger than twice the size of the sheets.

step two Couch the first sheet at one end of the cloth.

1 Have ready a large couching cloth on a felt pad or piece of blanket and pressing board. The pressing apparatus (boards, pads, and couching cloths) needs to be a little larger than twice the size of the mold and deckle you are using. Dip the mold and deckle into the vat of pulp, collecting a ⅛-inch layer of pulp on the mesh screen. You do not want to make each sheet too thick, as the laminating process will double the thickness of each page of the folder. Couch the first sheet onto one end of the cloth, steadying the base of the mold with one hand and turning the sheet face down onto the cloth with a rolling motion as though you are closing a book.

step three The frame of the mold acts as a spacer between the first and second sheets.

2 Continue the rolling motion to lift the mold away from the couched sheet, lifting the outer edge of the mold and keeping firm pressure on the inner edge as the pulp comes away from the mold to lie flat on the couching cloth.

You need to ensure that the first sheet is quite straight on the couching cloth, as the second sheet will need to be perfectly aligned with the first. If the first sheet is placed at too much of an angle, you may have difficulty aligning the second sheet (see following pages) so that all of its edges are within the couching cloth, felt mat, and pressing board sandwich.

3 Dip the mold and deckle into the vat of pulp again, collecting the same thickness of pulp. Drain off the water, shaking the mold gently to ensure the pulp settles evenly. Remove the deckle, and carefully place the edge of the mold next to the sheet that you have already placed on the couching cloth, taking care to align the second sheet exactly with the first. The frame of the mold will act as a spacer between the sheets, as you need to leave a gap of about 1¼–1⅜ inches between the pages. These two couched sheets form the base of a pair of laminated pages. You will now add the binding thread, which will be laminated between the sheets.

step four Cut two lengths of string and lay them across the couched sheets.

4 Cut thick string or very fine rope made of a natural material into two pieces, each 75 cm (29½ in) long. Hemp, sisal, linen, or cotton string is suitable for this project. Wool is not suitable, as it is too elastic. The more fibrous the string, the more securely it will be trapped in the laminated sheets, as the fibers of the paper pulp will become entangled with the fibers of the string.

Lay one piece of string across both of the couched sheets, 2 inches from the top edge, and another piece 2 inches from the bottom edge. There will be tails hanging over the edges, so take care not to catch or pull these at any time.

5 Dip the mold and deckle into the vat of pulp to make another sheet and couch it directly on top of the first sheet on the couching cloth. You will need to make sure that the top sheet is exactly aligned with the bottom sheet to create a perfect laminated sheet.

The string is now trapped between the two layers of pulp, ready for pressing. When the couched sheets are pressed together and allowed to dry, the string will become fused inside the paper covers of the folder.

step five Couch a new sheet on top of the first, trapping the string between the layers.

step six Repeat with a fourth sheet, then press and dry as usual.

6 Dip the mold and deckle into the vat of pulp again to create a fourth sheet. Couch this on top of the remaining bottom sheet, using the edge of the mold as a spacer as before and ensuring that the two layers of paper are exactly on top of each other.

7 Cover the completed sheets with another couching cloth, another felt pad or piece of blanket, and another pressing board. Use G-clamps to screw the sandwich together tightly and drain away excess liquid. The longer you can leave these sheets pressing, the better, as this will help the bonding.

8 Remove the G-clamps from the pressing sandwich and take off the top board and top blanket. Slide the two couching cloths with the stationery folder between them onto a drying board, taking care not to pull the strings as you move the assembly. The paper will dry while still between the two cloths. Allow the pages to completely dry before removing the top couching cloth by gently peeling it back. Turn the whole thing over and carefully peel the other cloth away from the folder.

Use this folder to hold stationery or pieces of handmade paper, or as a presentation pack for a gift.

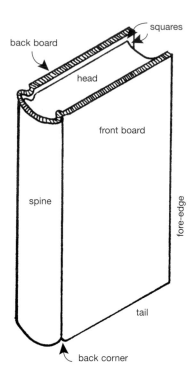

back board

squares

head

front board

spine

fore-edge

tail

back corner

Parts of a book

Head: The top of the book

Tail: The bottom of the book

Fore-edge: The front opening

Spine: The closed back edge, which
hides the sewing

Boards: The front and back covers
of a book

Endpapers: Folded folio attached to the
back and front boards and forming
the first sheet

Squares: The part of the cover board
that extends beyond the pasted down
endpaper, evenly on all four sides

Text: All the space between the covers
that is available for writing

Section: A group of folios sewn together
at the spine

Folio: Consists of two leaves or four
pages

Leaf: Consists of two pages; that is,
a front and back

Page: One side of a leaf

Handmade books

Sheets of paper, a needle and thread or some glue are all you need to create a simple book. Using your own handmade paper is the start of creating unique volumes: it becomes even more special when you add photographs, drawings or personal memorabilia in both images and words. You are limited only by your own imagination when it comes to book making. There are few things more rewarding than making a book that is personal to you or your family.

The instructions that follow start with very simple procedures and move on to a few that are a little more complex. Some of the books are fun books suitable for all ages to attempt, while others require absolute precision and a little dedication.

While books are made to convey information, the ideal book is one in which the appearance and contents work as one. In other words, you can create a book and then select suitable images to go inside, or you can have an idea about what words and images you want to put down on paper and create a binding to reflect your purpose.

While most of the books in this section are made with handmade paper, you can substitute commercially manufactured papers. Always choose papers carefully for quality, texture, and color. As is true in any craft, the best materials will always make the best product.

Paper grain

Handmade paper has little, if any, grain. Machine-made papers, however, have a tendency for the cellulose fibers to lie in the same direction. Paper will fold, crease, bend, and tear more easily along the grain. It is important that the grain of the paper should run from head to tail in books and cards.

When dampened, such as when glue is applied, paper will stretch against the grain, then shrink as it dries. When glued to a dry board the paper will force the board to curl as it shrinks; however, when a cover paper is placed on one side of a board and an endpaper on the other, the shrinkage on one side is balanced by the shrinkage on the other, providing they are glued with the grain facing in the same direction. This is why books should be pressed under a heavy weight as they dry.

Testing for grain direction

Bend the paper horizontally and apply light pressure with your hand in a bouncing fashion. Then bend the paper vertically and again apply light pressure with your hand in the same manner. The bend that gives less resistance indicates the grain direction. Alternatively, take a small section of the paper and fold it both horizontally and vertically—he crisper fold indicates the grain direction—or moisten a small section of paper, which will curl slightly: the grain runs along the hollow of the curl.

Adhesives

Paste is made of wheat flour, cornstarch, or starch. Paste is soluble in water and is one of the most acceptable adhesives for most bookbinding jobs, including conservation work. A recipe for paste is given at right.

White school glue is a surface glue. It dries quickly and therefore does not give much margin for error, such as adjusting endpapers. This glue should be applied as a thin even coating and is ideal for covering boards and tipping in.

Tipping in

Tipping in is the process of applying glue to the edge of a piece of paper, such as the folded edge of endpapers or the narrow overlap for joining lengths of paper for a concertina. Use a piece of wastepaper as a mask to allow the glue to be applied close to the edge.

To make your own paste

6 tablespoons wheat flour or cornstarch
2 cups water
OR approximately one part starch to six parts water

Mix the dry material in a little water to make a smooth paste. Add the remaining water.

Cook over a very low heat or in a double saucepan, stirring constantly to avoid lumps. Bring to the boil and allow to simmer for a few minutes while constantly stirring.

Allow to cool. Add a little water to the top to avoid a skin forming. Place in the refrigerator and take out only as much as you need and discard any excess when you are finished. Do not return the paste you are using to the batch in the refrigerator. Paste will keep a few days in the refrigerator.

Paste is ideal to use when adding endpapers as it allows time to rectify mistakes. Always dry pasted paper under weights.

Hint

If you intend making a few books, it is a good idea to make a sample book to keep for reference, in which you can add some notes about problems you encountered or ideas about what you could put in the book. This can act as a sort of reference library.

Examples of books with simple tab covers, as explained on page 87.

Concertina books

The concertina, which traditionally is an oriental binding, provides one of the most versatile formats for the construction of artists' books. As it is a continuous length of paper, both the front and back of the pages can be used for text and images. A concertina book can be allowed to lie flat and closed, or to stand open and reveal its contents at a glance.

The concertina can also be used to form a narrow spine onto which pages can be sewn, either in the valleys or on the hills of the concertina. The use of colored threads to attach the pages to the concertina spine can create decorative finishes to the spine. For stitching directions, see the section on simple sewn books, pages 84–87.

As a decorative alternative, you can make a second concertina spine of contrasting color or texture to slip over the one forming the spine of the book. The ends of the decorative cover slip into the front and back covers of the triple-fold book (see the project on page 60).

Concertina, or accordion, books must have an even number of sections and the grain of the paper (see page 52) should run from head to tail of the book to allow for crisp folds. There are several methods of folding concertina books, but the most important aspect of a concertina book is that each fold must lie exactly on top of the one below. The size of the book is determined by the desired height of the book and the width of the pages, multiplied by the number of sections required; for example, a book 5 inches in height with eight sections of 3½-inch-wide pages requires paper measuring 5 x (3½ x 8) inches (that is, 5 x 28 inches).

Eight-fold concertina book

This basic concertina book can be decorated with a variety of cover treatments.

1 Fold the strip of paper exactly in half by placing the right-hand edge precisely on top of the left-hand edge. Make a sharp fold using a bone folder. This creates what is known as a valley fold, with the crease on the outside or back of the paper.

2 Open the paper and place the left-hand edge on the center valley fold, then bring the right-hand edge and place it on the valley fold. Use a bone folder to press down the two new folds on the left and right. Open the paper. You will now have three valley folds.

3 Place the right-hand edge of the paper to lie exactly along the edge of the right-hand valley fold, as shown in the diagram below. Press down the new fold created between the edge of the paper and the first valley fold. This creates the first hill fold. Repeat on the left-hand side of the book. Turn the paper over.

4 Place the outer right-hand edge of the paper exactly along the center valley fold. Press down the new fold created between the first and second valley folds. You will now have two hill folds on this side of the book. Repeat on the left-hand side.

5 Finally, fold the first valley fold inward to create the complete concertina. It is essential that all edges—top, bottom, and sides—line up exactly. The first and last pages will be attached to a hard cover (see page 58) or slipped into the front and back covers of the double-fold or triple-fold covers (see pages 59–61).

For a longer concertina (with more pages), you may add extra paper by gluing two or more strips together. The joins should be made at a hill or valley fold. Allow ¼ inch extra for overlapping. (See directions for "Tipping in" on page 53.)

Materials

5 x 28-inch strip
   of paper

Tools

Bone folder
Glue

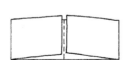

step one Fold the paper exactly in half.

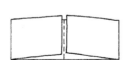

step two Fold the edges to meet at the center.

step three Create a hill fold on each side.

step four Fold the outer edges to the center.

step five Complete the concertina.

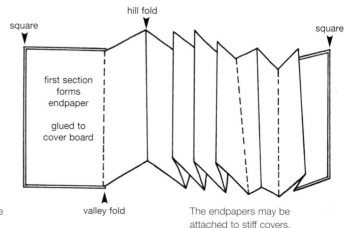

first section forms endpaper

glued to cover board

hill fold

square

square

valley fold

The endpapers may be attached to stiff covers.

Materials

Two pieces of 1/32-inch thick cardboard (with grain running head to tail), 5¹⁵⁄₁₆ x 4 ¼ inches; this fits an A6 concertina and gives 1/32-inch squares (see Parts of a book, page 52). If using a format other than A6, you will require cardboard 1/16 inch longer and wider than the concertina booklet

Two pieces of decorative paper approximately 1¼ inches longer and wider than the cardboard covers

Clean wastepaper, for masking when gluing

Tools

Bone folder

White school glue and brush

Soft cloth

Craft knife or paper scissors

Heavy weight or book press

Cover variations
Hard cover

1 Ensure the cardboard covers are square at the corners. With the cardboard lying on a piece of wastepaper, apply a thin, even coat of glue all over the front cover. Discard the wastepaper (to prevent any glue being accidentally transferred to the outside of the cover paper as you work on subsequent steps). Center the front cover with the glued side facing down on the wrong side of the decorative cover paper. Press the cardboard onto the cover paper. Turn it over and rub down with a soft cloth or a bone folder to ensure there are no air bubbles trapped between the cover paper and the cardboard. Turn the cover over again and cut a triangular section from each corner that finishes approximately 3 mm (⅛ in) from the corner of the cover board.

2 With the cover lying face down on a clean piece of wastepaper, apply glue to the top and bottom edges of the cover paper where it extends beyond the cardboard cover. Turn the paper over onto the cardboard and rub with a bone folder. Discard the wastepaper.

3 At each corner, use the bone folder to pull down any excess paper that might

protrude when the sides are turned over the edges of the cardboard. (See the diagram below.)

4 Taking a new piece of clean wastepaper, apply glue to the side edges of the cover paper that extend beyond the cardboard. Turn the cover paper onto the cardboard and rub down with a bone folder. Discard the wastepaper. Repeat this process for the back cover of the book.

5 Place a piece of wastepaper between the first and second sections of the concertina, and another piece of wastepaper between the second and third sections. This will prevent glue accidentally getting onto other pages of the concertina.

6 To attach the covers, apply a light, even coating of glue all over the front of the first section of the concertina. Discard the wastepaper and line up the book over the reverse of the front cover, making sure it is well centered, with the same amount of cover board showing on all sides around the pages of the book. Rub down the glued section with a soft cloth or bone folder to ensure there are no air bubbles. Repeat to attach the back cover.

7 Place the book under a heavy weight or in a book press and allow the glue to dry overnight before using.

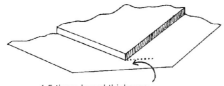

1.5 times board thickness

step one Cut a triangle from each corner of the cover paper.

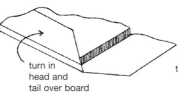

turn in head and tail over board

step two Fold the cover paper over the edge of the cardboard.

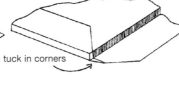

tuck in corners

step three Use a bone folder to crease excess paper at the corners.

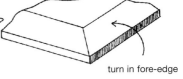

turn in fore-edge

step four Turn over the side edges of the cover paper.

tep two Fold the side edges toward the center fold.

step three Slip the endpapers of the concertina book inside the pockets.

Double-fold cover

1 Place the sheet of paper horizontally on the work surface in front of you. Fold the bottom edge up to the middle of the page and the top edge down to the middle of the page. The two edges should almost meet at the midpoint of the page.

2 Fold the paper in half vertically. This fold creates the spine of the book cover. Fold the right-hand and left-hand edges in to almost meet at the center fold. Crease with a bone folder.

3 To attach the cover to the book, slip the right-hand end of the concertina into the pocket created by the right-hand fold, and the left-hand end of the concertina into the pocket created by the left-hand fold.

Folding an A3 sheet in this manner creates a cover to hold an A5-size booklet. You can make the folds smaller to accommodate a larger book, or use an A4 sheet for a much smaller book.

Materials
One sheet of A3 (11¾ x 16½ inch) paper

Tools
Bone folder

Materials

The following dimensions fit
   an A6 (4⅛ x 5¹³⁄₁₆ inch)
   booklet; that is, A5 (5¹³⁄₁₆ x
   8¼ inch) paper folded in
   half. The completed cover
   measures 6 x 4¼ inches

Two pieces of medium-weight
   paper such as Canson
   Mi-Teintes, each 15¹⁵⁄₁₆ x
   11 inches; that is, ¹⁄₁₆ inch
   longer than the height of
   the A6 book and almost
   three times its width

Two pieces of medium-weight
   paper in a contrasting color,
   each 16½ x 4¼ inches;
   that is, a little less than
   three times the height of
   the book times the width
   of the cover

Use the contrasting color to
   create a spine if required.
   You will need a piece of
   paper 5¹⁵⁄₁₆ x 4¾ inches;
   that is, the height of the
   cover times approximately
   2¼ inches wide to slip into
   the front and back covers

Tools

Bone folder
Glue and applicator brush,
   if desired

step one Fold the cover paper around the contrasting paper strip.

Triple-fold cover

1 Position a strip of contrasting paper
vertically in the center of a strip of cover
paper and fold the left and right sides
of the cover paper to fit neatly over
the contrasting paper, as shown in the
photograph above. Center the folded cover
paper on the contrasting strip and fold the
ends of the contrasting strip over to fit
neatly around the cover paper.

2 Unfold and remove the contrasting strip,
but leave the cover paper folded. Turn
the cover paper over, and with the flaps
of the cover paper facing away from you

step three Insert the endpaper of the concertina book into the pocket.

and the flaps of the contrasting paper toward you, slip the top section of the contrasting paper into the space between the flaps of the cover paper and its center panel. Now slip the bottom flap of the contrasting paper into the other end of the cover paper pocket. If you find it difficult to slip the two sections together, you can trim a tiny tapered sliver from each side of the flaps of contrasting paper.

3 Repeat this process with the remaining paper strips to make the back cover of the book. Slip the endpapers of the concertina book under the contrasting paper strips of both front and back covers.

4 To make a spine for your book, score a line down the middle of the spine paper strip. Depending of the thickness of your book, you may need to score another line to the right or left of the first one. Crease a fold on each scored line and slip one side of the fold into the front cover and the other side into the back cover, beside the end papers of the book. Although it is not strictly necessary, you can carefully add a dab of glue to secure the spine in place.

Interlocking concertina book

This double concertina book comprises a large concertina of medium- to heavyweight paper, which acts as a support for the smaller one, of medium-weight paper, on which images and text are featured.

The dimensions for this book can be altered provided you keep the same proportions. The large concertina has eight sections into which are cut six windows. The smaller concertina is threaded through these windows and when the book is closed it sits neatly within the windows cut into the larger concertina. The smaller concertina has ten sections, eight of which sit within the window area as described, and two sections that are attached to the first and last sections of the larger concertina.

Materials
Large concertina: medium- to heavyweight paper 10¾ x 30¾ inches
Small concertina: medium-weight paper 5⅛ x 24¾ inches
Two cover boards 4⅛ x 11 inches
Cover paper (the example pictured uses the same paper as used for the small concertina)
Suitable materials for images (paint, pastel, ink, or photographs)
Clean wastepaper, for masking when gluing

Tools
Metal ruler
Sharp pencil
Craft knife
Dividers
Bone folder
Glue and glue brush

step two Three sections will form the flaps to which the smaller concertina is glued.

step four Thread the smaller concertina through the windows of the larger.

1 Fold the large concertina into eight sections (see instructions for eight-fold concertina on page 57). On sections two and seven of the concertina, measure 2⅛ inches down from the top of the paper. Draw a light pencil line connecting these points from section two to section seven to act as a guide for cutting the windows. From this line measure down 5⅛ inches and draw another light pencil line. Measure in ⅜ inch from the right-hand fold and the left-hand fold on each of sections two to seven. Make a light pencil mark to join the top and bottom lines, creating the cutting lines for six windows on these center sections of the concertina.

2 On sections three, five, and seven, cut out and remove the window completely. On the remaining sections—two, four and six—cut along the top, right-hand side, and bottom lines only. Score a line down the middle of each flap and turn it backwards, as shown in the photograph above. Trim a tapered sliver from the right-hand corner of each flap up to the fold on both the top and bottom of the flap. This will prevent the flap from showing above the smaller concertina when it is attached.

3 Mark the center of the paper to be used for the smaller concertina and, using dividers, mark four sections to the right

step five Mask with wastepaper and glue the flap.

step six Align the edge of the large concertina carefully over the glued flap and press.

of the center and four sections to the left of the center. The measurement for the sections of the smaller concertina should be about 1/32 inch smaller than the window in the larger concertina, so that the eight sections of the smaller concertina will fit neatly within the windows when the book is closed. You will have small sections left over at the beginning and end of the smaller concertina (see Step 6).

4 Before folding the smaller concertina, complete your artwork, adding images or text, as you desire. Fold the small concertina and thread it through the windows of the larger concertina.

5 With the concertinas lying face down, work from right to left, applying a thin layer of glue to the outer half of each flap. Line up the edge of the flap with the folded edge of the corresponding section of the small concertina. Rub down with the bone folder.

6 Close both concertinas. Open the first section of the larger concertina to reveal the front flap of the smaller concertina. Use a piece of wastepaper to protect the smaller concertina as you apply glue to the back of the flap. Close the large concertina carefully, rubbing it down over the glued flap. Turn the book over and repeat for the last flap of the smaller concertina.

Hints

Place the double concertina book under a heavy weight or in a book press to dry overnight. Cover the front and back boards with selected paper (as described on page 58). Attach the front and back covers to the first and last sections of the larger concertina. Once again, place under a weight overnight and, if desired, decorate the front cover to indicate the contents of the book.

Star book

This clever contraption offers a variation on paper folding, and will give an opportunity to showcase handmade or commercially manufactured decorative papers.

Squares of paper ingeniously folded make up the pages of this project, which adds a surprising twist to the idea of a book. The example shown here is very small, but the same technique can easily be used to make a larger version.

Materials

Nine squares of paper in at least two colors

Two pieces of matt board or similar thickness of card stock for cover. The size should be ⅜-inch larger than the square paper folded into quarters

Clean wastepaper, for masking when gluing

Two pieces of decorative paper 1⅛ inches larger than the cardboard covers

Two pieces of ⅛-inch ribbon, 10 inches long

Tools

Bone folder

Glue and brush

step one Crease the square along both horizontal axes.

step two Turn the square over and crease along one diagonal axis.

1 The squares of paper used for the pages of the star book in these photographs measure approximately 3 inches square. This creates a compact book. Larger or smaller squares may be used, as desired. Begin with a square of paper, right side facing up. Fold the square in half horizontally, and then open it out. Turn it 90 degrees and fold it in half horizontally again. Press the creases with your fingertip as shown in the photograph.

2 Open the paper out and turn it over so the wrong side is facing up. Fold the paper along one diagonal axis and press the crease with your fingertip.

3 Open the paper out with the wrong side still facing up, and gently push the center point from underneath with one finger. This allows you to bring the two points of the diagonal fold together so that they meet in the middle, with one square face upward, and another square face on the bottom of the folded piece.

4 Repeat this folding process with the remaining squares of both types of paper, until you have the required number of folded squares. The pictured example uses nine, but if you want more, simply continue folding until you have the desired number of pages for your book.

step three Push the center upward, bringing the points of the diagonal fold together.

step five Alternate the colors and direction of the folded squares.

5 When joining the folded squares, it is best to be methodical. Firstly sort the pages by color or texture, ensuring that the two different papers you have used alternate with each other. You may, of course, use more than two different papers, arranging the folded squares in any pattern you prefer. Next, you need to arrange the pages for gluing, so that the openings alternate in direction; that is, every second page has the enclosed or "blind" corner facing toward you, and every other page is rotated 180 degrees so that the opening flap corner faces you. You will glue the bottom square face of one page to the top square face of the next in the order you have planned.

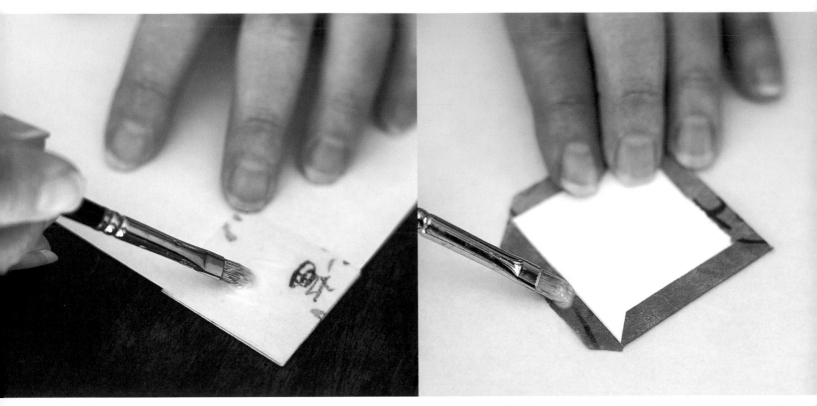

step six Use wastepaper as a mask when applying glue to the folded pages.

step seven Glue the cover paper over the boards to create hard covers for the book

6 When gluing the pages together, slip the corner of a sheet of clean wastepaper inside the folded square and apply glue to the bottom square face of the first folded page. Discard the wastepaper, and carefully place the top square face of the second folded page on top of this, ensuring that the blind corner of the first page aligns with the open corner of the second. Rub with a bone folder to eliminate air bubbles, then turn the assembly over and insert a new sheet of wastepaper inside the bottom face of the second page to apply glue as before. Continue in this manner until all of the pages are glued together in alternate directions and with alternate colors.

Glue ribbon inside the cover boards.

Ensure that the ribbons hang free in the same direction.

7 Apply glue to the front of one cover board and center it on a square of decorative cover paper. Turn it over and use a bone folder or a soft cloth to smooth out any air bubbles. Cut a triangle off each corner of the cover paper to miter the corners before turning. Working on wastepaper, apply glue to the flaps and turn them over onto the inside of the cover board. Glue and turn one flap at a time for best results. Repeat to create the back cover of the book.

8 Place a length of narrow ribbon on the inside of each cover board, with the end of the ribbon in the center of the board. Glue the ribbon in place. If the paper you have used for the book covers has an obvious right way up, you will need to be careful that the ribbons are oriented correctly before you glue them in place.

9 Finally, glue the assembled pages to the inside of one cover, then the other, ensuring that the ribbons hang free in the same direction. Place your book under a heavy weight or in a book press overnight to allow the glue to dry. When you remove it, wrap the ribbons around the book and tie them to keep the book closed. If you wish, add a decorative bead, knot, or charm to the ends of the ribbons, as shown in the example of this book on pages 66–67.

Concertina cardholder

Artists' trading cards (ATCs) are worked in paper, fabric, and other materials and exchanged between artists or friends. This is an excellent way of learning new decorative skills and techniques in your chosen field of craft and outside it. Storing these cards in an attractive and portable manner is another way of expanding your skill base. This concertina book incorporates pockets that are suitable to hold trading cards—fill the pockets with those you have received, or those you have made and are ready to swap.

This folder could also be used for standard business cards, photos, or mementos. Check that the dimensions of the cardholder will accommodate the intended contents; if not, adjust the measurements.

Materials
Heavy tracing paper, at least 12 x 32 inches
Four buttons
Strong sewing thread

Tools
Long metal ruler
Bone folder or plastic knife
Self-healing cutting mat (preferably with a grid marked on it to aid with alignment)
Awl
Needle

step one Use a metal ruler to keep the paper firm as you fold on the scored line.

step two Flatten each fold with a bone folder to give a sharp crease.

1 Cut a piece of paper 30 x 80 cm (12 x 32 in). Fold it in half lengthwise. Mark 5.5 cm (2¼ in) from the top edge and score a line with the bone folder. Using a ruler to keep the paper firm and guide you, fold the top edge of the paper toward the center fold along this line. Flatten the crease with the bone folder. Turn the paper over and repeat on the other side.

2 To make the concertina, divide the length of the paper into 16 equal parts (in this case, 5 cm, or 2 in, each). Score a line with the bone folder from top to bottom to assist folding. Fold alternate hill and valley folds (see page 57) along the scored lines,

flattening each fold with the bone folder as you go. You may find it easier when making the concertina if you fold the center fold first, and work on one side, then the other, as described in the instructions on page 57.

3 When all folds are completed, you can either close off the ends of the pockets on the first and last sections of the book, or leave them open. In this example a button has been stitched to the outer end, which serves as a decorative element as well as a means of tying the book closed. Pierce stitching holes through the paper with an awl before stitching the button on, using strong sewing thread and a paper needle.

step three Sew on buttons to secure the open ends of the pockets.

step four Use twine or ribbon to hold the book closed when it is not on display.

4 Fill front and back pockets with trading cards, photos or any interesting pieces you may have collected. The book stands nicely on its own as a display book, but if you want to store or carry it, use the buttons to attach lengths of narrow ribbon or twine and secure the pages closed.

Variations

You can easily change the dimensions of this book, bearing in mind that you need a reasonable length of paper to make sixteen pages. If your paper is too short, you can join it on a fold, allowing extra length for the overlap, or you can make a book with fewer pages. For example, you can divide the length by twelve or eight instead of sixteen.

Lightweight card stock, such as Canson Mi-Teintes, can be used instead of tracing paper, but avoid thick papers as they are too difficult to fold.

Photo album

The concertina, as well as acting as the pages of a book, can also act as a binding to which pages are sewn or glued. When the pages are sewn to the concertina they can be attached to either the valley or the hill folds.

In creating this photograph album, the pages are glued to the concertina spine. The concertina compensates for the thickness of the photographs when added to the pages and prevents swelling of the book at the fore-edge.

Materials

Concertina spine and endpapers:
    Canson Mi-Teintes or similar, 10¼ x
    29½ inches
Pages: ten sheets Canson 10¼ x 13¾ inches
Cover boards: two boards 7¼ x 10½ inches
    and ¹⁄₁₆ inch thick
Cover paper: two sheets of A4 (8¼ x 11¾ inch)
    handmade paper or other decorative paper
Front cover decoration: piece of gold paper
    as background; feathers, flowers, and other
    objects for collage; piece of clear acetate
    to cover decoration
Photographs

Tools

Dividers
Bone folder
White school glue and applicator brush
Craft knife
Metal ruler
Cutting mat
Double-sided adhesive tape

step three Glue the last concertina section to the back of a page.

1 Fold the spine paper in half. Use dividers to mark off, on the top and bottom edges, ten sections to the left of the center fold and ten sections to the right of the center fold at ¾ inch intervals. Score and fold the valley and hill folds as described on page 57. You now have ten concertinas, which take up 15 inches of the spine paper. The remaining paper—7 inches on the left and 7 inches on the right—will be used as endpapers to attach the completed album to the cover boards.

2 Score a line down the center of each of the 10 pages and fold to create double pages measuring 10¼ x 7 inches. Rub down the crease with a bone folder to give a crisp fold. The fold will be the fore-edge of the album, while the open ends will be glued to the concertina spine.

3 Apply glue to the right-hand side of the last concertina section (not to the endpaper). Place the back inside edge of one of the folded pages into the valley fold and press the glued side of the concertina on to the page. Do not attach the front of the page at this stage. Continue fixing the pages to the right-hand sides of the concertina until all ten folded pages have their back sections glued to the right-hand sides of the concertina sections.

ep six Turn the cover paper to the back of the window and glue down the edges.

step seven Attach the collage behind the window with double-sided adhesive tape.

4 Place the front sections of each page on the left-hand sections of the concertina, but do not glue them. Cut windows in the pages slightly smaller than the size of the photograph you wish to display. Attach the photograph behind the window with double-sided adhesive tape. Once the photographs have been attached to both the front and back of each page in this manner, glue the edge of the front section of the page to the left-hand side of the concertina.

5 Cut a window for your collage in the front cover board. On a piece of gold paper, add decoration. Alternatively, use a photograph. Overlay clear acetate for protection.

6 Cover the back and front cover boards with paper, following the instructions on page 58. Where the window is cut in the front board make two diagonal cuts in the paper from the top to bottom corners. Trim away the points of the four triangles thus formed, leaving about ⅜ inch of paper to turn to the back and glue down.

7 Attach your collage to the back of the window with double-sided adhesive tape. Center the cover boards over the album. Place wastepaper between the endpaper and the album, as you apply glue to the end paper and place the board in position. Place the book under a weight to dry overnight.

Hints

When working with precious heirlooms such as photographs, it is important to create an acid-free environment to prevent deterioration of the archival material. Choose acid- and lignin-free paper, adhesives, and embellishments wherever possible. Ask at your art and craft supplies store or read the manufacturer's instructions to determine whether your materials are acid free.

Double concertina with paper cutouts

This book design is based on a concertina with a wedge removed from the center. Either handmade or commercially manufactured papers can be used. If desired, the paper can be color-washed or sprayed with ink before beginning (the example shown here was colored using tea bags).

If using handmade papers, they will need to be joined to make a sheet of sufficient size. Join them neatly by tipping in along the concertina folds so that the joins are less visible.

Materials

Handmade or watercolor paper cut
   to 11½ x 31½ inches
Contrasting paper for cutout patterns
White school glue

Tools

Bone folder
Metal ruler
Scissors

step one Create an eight-section concertina fold.

step four Cut out and discard the central triangle.

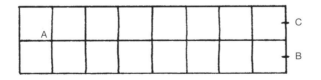

diagram A Marking points A, B, and C.

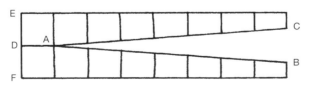

diagram B Folding along the line D–A.

1 Color both sides of the paper, if desired, and allow to dry. With the right side facing and starting with a valley fold, fold the whole sheet accurately into an eight-page concertina (follow the instructions on page 57). Crease well, rubbing the folds with a bone folder to make sharp creases.

2 Flatten out the concertina, then fold the paper down the center lengthwise, as shown in Diagram A at left. Crease well, then unfold the paper again.

3 On the right-hand end, mark a point 7.5 cm (3 in) up from the bottom right-hand corner (marked B on Diagram A). Mark

ep five Fold the concertina in half at the center point along line D–A.

step seven Cut out symmetrical patterns in contrasting paper to decorate.

another point 7.5 cm (3 in) down from the top right-hand corner (marked C).

4 Mark point A at the intersection of the first fold on the left-hand side and the horizontal center fold. Rule lines from this intersection (point A) to points B and C. This makes a large triangle in the center. Cut along the sides of this triangle (lines B–A and C–A) and remove it.

5 Fold along the line D–A, as marked in Diagram B, bringing point E to point F. Then refold the book in concertina style from A to B and from A to C.

6 You will now have a double concertina with a high center fold and tapered arms. The two arms of the concertina become smaller as they get closer to the ends.

7 Take some contrasting handmade paper, and cut shapes that will fit onto the pages of the concertina book. The shapes may be all the same size, or may be the same width but different heights to accommodate the declining heights of the concertina pages. Fold the shapes into quarters and cut out small segments to create decorative, symmetrical designs. Unfold the shapes and glue them to the concertina pages.

Simple sewn books

The pamphlet, or single-section book using a three- or five-hole sewing, is the simplest introduction to basic bookbinding techniques. This type of binding relies on sewing alone; no glue is used. Although the method of sewing is simple, it allows for many variations because sewing can commence from the inside or the outside of the book. By finishing the sewing on the outside, decorative finishes can be made on the spine, such as a bow, fringing, or the addition of beads. Colored threads to tone or contrast with the covers could also be used.

Materials
Paper for text: experiment with various weights, textures and don't be afraid to use different papers, both commercial and handmade, in a single book
Decorative paper for endpapers—decorative papers can also strengthen covers
Card stock or heavyweight paper for covers
Decorative sewing thread or waxed linen thread

Tools
Cutting knife
Self-healing cutting mat
Metal ruler
Pencil
Awl
Needle

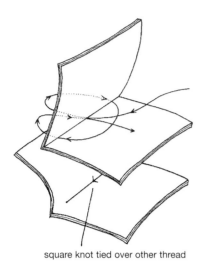

square knot tied over other thread

diagram 1 Three-hole sewing, with the knot inside the pages.

diagram 2 Five-hole sewing, with the knot on the outside of the book.

Hints

Use a longer thread and begin sewing from the outside of the spine. Add beads or buttons to the ends of the threads.

Use two or three colored threads and braid the ends. Tie a knot just short of the end of the thread and fringe the section of the thread after the knot.

Sew with fine ribbon or gold or silver thread. Tie off with a bow.

1 Cut paper to the size required for the folios of the book. Fold the folios in half and slip them inside one another to create a section. Usually eight to ten folios is sufficient for a small book, but the number of folios will also be determined by the weight of the paper; that is, thicker paper will allow fewer folios and thinner paper will allow more folios.

2 Place a decorative piece of paper, the same size as the folios, on the outside of the section to act as endpapers. Cut a cover from card or heavy paper approximately $\frac{1}{16}$ inch longer and wider than the folios. This will allow narrow squares around the outer edges of the book. Place the cover in position on the outside of the folded folios.

3 To mark the sewing stations, open the book to the middle. Place a light pencil mark in the center of the folded spine. Place a second pencil mark between the first mark and the head (top) of the book. Then place a pencil mark between the first pencil mark and the tail (bottom) of the book. This marks the sewing stations for a pamphlet or three-hole sewing (see Diagram 1). This is ideal for small books but larger books may require a five-hole (see Diagram 2) or even a seven-hole sewing. The sewing procedure is the same in all cases. The diagrams above left show three- and five-hole sewing, with the three-hole method shown beginning from inside the book, while the five-hole method is illustrated beginning from the outside of the book. You can begin either way, depending on whether you want the knotted ends to be visible on the spine (as in the photographs, above right).

4 With an awl or pointed tool, such as a compass, pierce through all pages and the cover at the marked sewing stations.

5 Cut a length of thread approximately three times the height of the book and begin sewing by inserting the needle into the center hole from the inside of the book. Pull the thread through to the back of the spine leaving about 6–8 cm (2½–3⅛ in) of thread on the inside to tie the final knot. Insert the needle into the top hole and pull through to the inside. Insert the needle into the bottom hole and pull through to the back. Insert the needle back into the center hole, ensuring the beginning and the end of the thread are on opposite sides of the long stitch that runs from the top sewing station to the bottom sewing station. It is essential to tie off the ends of the thread across the long thread that covers the center hole to prevent the knot from pulling through the center hole.

6 Cut a piece of decorative paper the same height as the card cover and approximately 3⅛–4 inches wider. Wrap the paper around the card cover and fold in the excess over the front and back cover at the fore-edge.

7 For a more secure covering, cut the decorative paper approximately 2½ inches longer and wider than the card cover. Center the open book on top of the reverse side of the decorative paper. Cut the corners of the decorative paper to miter them. Also cut a small V from the decorative paper at the head and tail of the spine to allow for the thickness of the pages. Turn over the edges of the decorative paper all around the card cover.

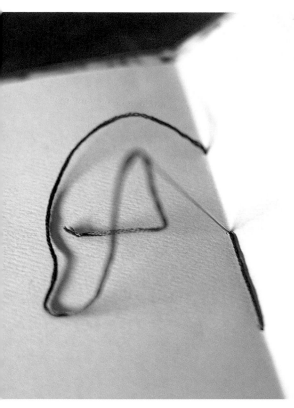

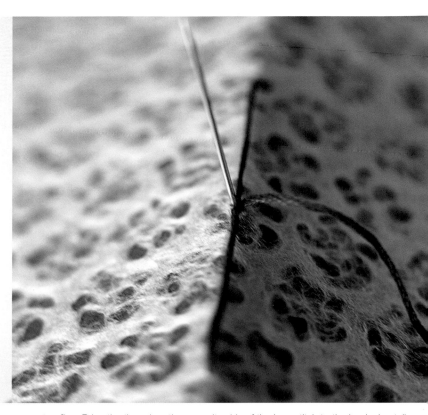

step five Take the thread back through the first sewing station.

step five Bring the thread on the opposite side of the long stitch to the beginning tail.

To avoid the use of adhesives, cut a small slot in the card cover which can lock over the decorative cover. An alternative method of securing the folded covers is to cut a tab on each corner of the folded-in sides (see Diagrams 3 and 4, at right). These tabs will slide into cuts made in the top and bottom folds of the cover.

8 A triple-fold cover (see page 60) may also be used. For a variation, use contrasting colored papers for the two folds and cut a decorative motif, such as a flower or a geometric design, out of the top fold so that the contrasting color shows through.

9 The double-fold cover, as described on page 59, can also be used as a cover to slip over sewn books.

Other variations

Cut slits into the card cover and weave contrasting paper through the slits. Rubber stamps or embroidery can also be used to decorate cover papers. Cut windows into the card cover and insert photos or other images (see page 79).

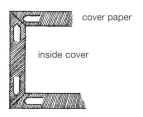

cover paper

inside cover

diagram 3 Tab closures at the top, bottom, and sides of cover paper

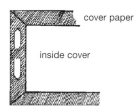

cover paper

inside cover

diagram 4 Tab closures at the sides of the cover paper only

Japanese-style stitched books

These books are based on the Japanese method of hand binding known as stab binding. In their traditional form, the pages are folded at the fore-edge and bound together by stitching over the spine edge, creating double pages. The covers are usually strong but flexible, and the head and tail of the spine are wrapped with a small piece of paper inside the binding for protection. As Chinese and Japanese scripts are written vertically and from right to left, the books open in reverse from Western-style books. The stitching on the outside of the spine becomes a feature of the book. The most common configuration is the four-hole style, but many holes can also be used and a great variety of stitching patterns is possible. Once you have started, you will want to keep experimenting and creating new stitching effects.

Materials to make an A6 (4⅛ x 5¹³⁄₁₆ inch) book

Approximately ten sheets of A5 (5¹³⁄₁₆ x 8¼ inch) handmade paper folded, or twenty sheets of A6 (4⅛ x 5¹³⁄₁₆ inch) paper

Two covers, A6 (4⅛ x 5¹³⁄₁₆ inch) size, slightly thicker or stronger than the pages, but not too stiff

30 inches strong thread, such as linen, embroidery cotton, narrow ribbon or string

Tools

Awl (or any sharp pointed tool for making holes)

Tapestry needle

Letter clips or bulldog clips

Four small scraps of waste cardboard to put under the clips

Wooden board or thick cardboard to support paper and protect work surface when making holes

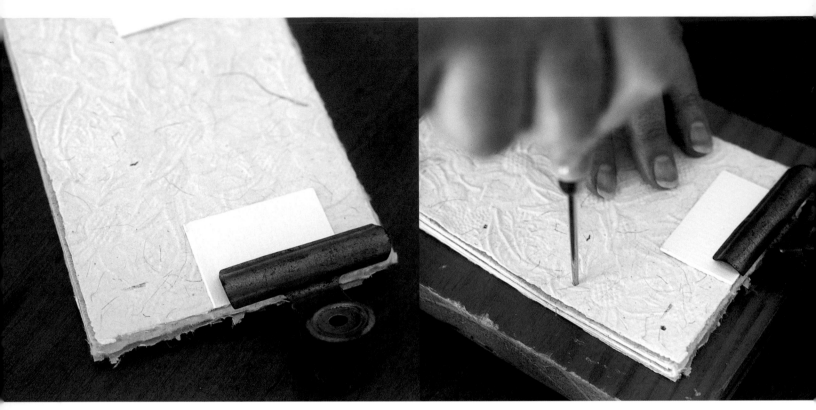

step one Clip pages together with a letter clip and some scrap card for protection.

step two Use an awl to make holes for stitching.

1 The photographs show pages that have been torn or have a deckle edge, giving a soft and natural appearance in keeping with the nature of handmade paper. Single A6 (4⅛ x 5¹³⁄₁₆ inch) pages are used, or you may fold A5 (5¹³⁄₁₆ x 8¼ inch) pages in half: the folded edges are sewn into the spine. Assemble the pages, lining them up evenly along the spine. Put covers in place. When satisfied with the positioning, clamp the pages together with letter clips, putting a small piece of cardboard under the clips to prevent indenting the pages.

2 Mark the positions for four holes, as shown in the photograph above. Place the assembled book on a board or thick card and make holes with the awl, holding it perfectly perpendicular to the board, not at an angle. Check that the holes are well defined on the reverse side. The holes must be large enough for the needle and thread to pass through several times.

3 With strong thread and a tapestry needle, start stitching at the third hole, from front to back. Leaving the tail of the thread hanging, take the needle through this hole, over the spine, and in through the same hole again to the back, pulling the thread firmly, but not too tight. Insert the needle up through the second hole and again over

ep three Pass the needle and thread through the head hole three times in all.

step four Add beads or buttons onto the tail of the thread as further decoration.

the spine and back through the same hole. The spine will start to feel firm. Continue to the first hole at the head of the book, where you will need to stitch over the spine, then back through the same hole again, over the head and back through the same hole again (passing the needle through the hole three times in all). Take the needle back through the second hole and then the third, filling in the spaces you left on the way up. Stitch the fourth hole the same way as the first hole, going over the spine and the tail, passing the needle three times into the same hole. Finish by coming back into the third hole where you started. Tie the two tail threads together.

4 Traditionally, the tail threads are concealed by burying them in the spine, but in this example the loose threads have been left outside after tying off to become another decorative feature. You may like to decorate the tail threads by attaching beads or buttons. Alternatively, these threads can be cut short, then fanned out by separating the fibers with a pin, or left long and adorned with buttons, shells, feathers, or other small trinkets. Since the stitching is an important feature of the book, it is worthwhile choosing a thread that complements your covers, either by matching or contrasting with their color and texture.

Hints

Stitching sounds complicated, but it is very logical, as you just keep going from one hole to the next, and as long as you don't skip any holes, you will always fill in the spaces on the way back. More adventurous embroiderers can experiment with fancy stitches. You can also try incorporating beading in the stitching.

Depending where you want the decorative tail to hang, you can start from any hole, and also choose between front or back.

Stick book

This book looks good if created using papers with a plant fiber content, as the deckle edges are then quite ragged. If making your own papers for this book, use a deckle alone, without the mold, to give the ragged effect. If you want to tear commercially manufactured paper to give a deckle edge, fold the paper on the tearing line, wet it with a paintbrush and gently pull the paper apart.

The binding of this book uses a stick instead of stitched thread. Alternatively, you could use metal or wooden bars.

Materials
Approximately 100 sheets of A5 ($5^{13}/_{16}$ x
    $8^{1}/_{4}$ inch) paper
Linen thread
Beeswax
Two strong sticks, about $6^{1}/_{4}$ inches long

Tools
Awl
Long needle

step one Use an awl to punch two holes in each sheet of paper.

step two Run linen thread through beeswax to lubricate it.

1 Use an awl to punch two holes in one end of each sheet, then place the sheets on top of one another so that the holes are aligned.

2 Run some linen thread through beeswax and thread a long needle. The wax makes the thread stronger.

3 Place one of the sticks across the holes on the front of the pile of paper, and the other stick across the holes on the back. From the back, push the needle through one of the holes, leaving about 4 inches of thread dangling at the back.

4 Bring the needle out on the front, then go around the stick and down the same hole to come out at the back. Make sure that the threads at the back are on either side of the stick. See the diagrams at right.

5 Tie with two knots and thread the ends into the needle. Push the needle into the hole and come out in the middle of the book (finishing off the threads in the middle of the book ensures that they are less visible). Snip off about 2.5 cm (1 in) from the hole.

6 Do the same with the other hole, attaching the sticks at both the back and front of the book.

step four Bring the needle around the stick and back through the same hole.

step five Take the tails of thread to the inside of the book to hide them.

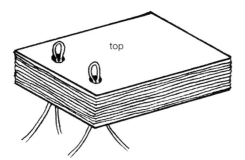

diagram 1 Thread goes around the stick (not shown)

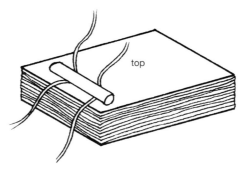

diagram 2 Tails should be either side of the stick.

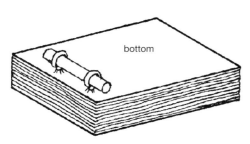

diagram 3 The finished book, secured with sticks.

Hints

This book is made mainly for show; with so many pages, it is too bulky for normal use. The rough edges are its feature. It has no cover, but if you wish to add one, it may help to score a line with a bone folder from head to tail a little distance from the stitch line. This will allow the book to open more easily.

A similar book can be made by making two holes and simply securing a button, bead, or both on either side as you go from front to back.

Torn book

Two types of torn and layered paper give an ethereal quality to this artistic book. Similar tones give a unified look, or you could consider using paper in a variety of hues that will be glimpsed through the tracing-paper windows.

Materials

Ten sheets of tracing paper,
   10 x 15 inches
Ten sheets handmade paper,
   8 x 15 inches
Artists' canvas, 10¾ x
   28 inches

Tools

Paper clips
Sewing machine and thread
Small paper scissors
   (optional)

1 Using one sheet of the handmade paper, tear it once lengthwise in a pleasing design. Place this onto one side of the tracing paper, aligning the top and bottom of the handmade paper pieces with the top and bottom of the tracing paper, thus leaving a gap between the two handmade paper pieces, as shown in the photograph at left. Secure with paper clips.

2 Set your sewing machine to a wide zigzag stitch. Sew the two papers together about ⅜ inch in from the edges of the handmade paper. Leave the ends of the threads dangling about by 4 inches if you want a shaggy look.

3 Turn the page over and, by cutting with small scissors or tearing, remove some of the excess tracing paper, being careful not to go too close to the stitches.

4 Repeat for all the sheets of handmade paper, varying the number of torn pieces on the page if desired. Fold the pages in half and create a book by your preferred stitching method.

5 The cover, of artists' canvas, can be made in one piece or in two pieces joined lengthwise and sewn using a decorative machine stitch. Fray the top and bottom edges of the canvas. Turn each end under ¾ inch and sew using a zigzag stitch.

6 Mark fold lines 10¾ inches in from each end and one vertically down the center. Iron them well and leave to cool.

7 Using a sharp pencil, mark the lines where the pages will be sewn. These will be ⅜ inch apart and will start 10⅝ inches from the outside fold lines.

8 Fold all the pages down the center and crease well. It may help if you cover the fold with some silicone paper and run a bone folder along the crease.

9 Lay the fold of one page onto the first sewing line and hold it in place with paper clips. Sew using a fairly long straight stitch, again leaving 4 inch tails of thread if you want a shaggy look; otherwise, trim them. Sew all pages in this manner.

Small chunky collage book

Collect interesting bits and pieces for the collages in this book—such things as pieces of jewelry, beads, pressed leaves and flowers, twigs, postage stamps, snippets of handmade paper, fabric, pieces of metal, leather, or anything else that will fit within the pages. Use white school glue or another adhesive that will secure the items to the pages. Alternatively, sew the collage items to the pages using strong thread.

To make the pages, spray a large sheet of commercially manufactured brown paper with ink (the pictured example uses walnut ink) and allow it to dry.

Materials
Concertina: brown paper, at least 14 inches
    wide and 29 inches long
Cover: decorative paper at least 12 x 14 inches
Open-weave cotton fabric, such as cheesecloth
Collage materials, as desired
Linen thread
Beeswax
Scrap card stock for sewing template

Tools
Metal ruler
Pencil
Craft knife
Glue
Awl
Tapestry needle
Bone folder
Paper clips

1 From the brown paper sheet, cut three strips each 4½ x 29 inches. On one end of each strip, fold in ⅝ inch and crease. On one of the pieces, cut off the folded end. Fold each piece into an eight-fold concertina, as explained on page 57. On the strips with the folded ends, measure the sections evenly from the creases, rather than the end of the strip.

2 Glue the three strips together, applying a thin layer of glue to the folded ends and sticking these to the edge of the next strip. When this process is complete, you will have one long concertina book of 24 pages.

3 To make the cover, cut a piece of decorative paper 6⅞ x 13⅜ inches and draw a pencil line all around the paper, 1 inch from each edge on the wrong side of the paper. Cut a piece of cheesecloth fabric to 4¾ x 11⅜ inches. Glue this to the center of the cover paper, on the wrong side and inside the pencil line. Press in a book press or under a heavy weight to flatten it out and allow the glue to dry.

4 At each corner, cut off a triangular piece as shown in the photograph of step three. Fold the edges over and glue them down. Press and allow to dry.

Glue endpapers inside the cover, over the fabric.

step eight Sew the concertina pages to the cover.

5 Cut another piece of the cover paper 4½ x 11 inches. Glue this to the inside of the cover. Dry and press. You will now have a cover that measures 4⅞ x 11⅜ inches.

6 Make a sewing template for the spine: on a piece of scrap card, draw a rectangle 3⅜ x 4⅞ inches. Across the top (the shorter measurement), and starting from the left, mark six points each ¼ inch apart. From the right, do the same. The middle space will be slightly larger than all the others. Draw a perpendicular line from each of these points to the bottom edge of the card.

7 Mark three dots evenly along each line, as shown in the diagram at right, and make holes using an awl. Line up the center point of the template and the center of the cover, holding the pieces together with paper clips. Using a sharp pencil, transfer the holes from the template to the cover.

8 Sew the concertina pages to the cover using the three-hole pamphlet stitch (see page 86) and waxed linen thread, stitching each valley fold to one line of holes. If desired, you can add further lightweight pages inside the concertina folds, as shown in the photograph above. Simply fold the paper and stitch it in as you sew the spine.

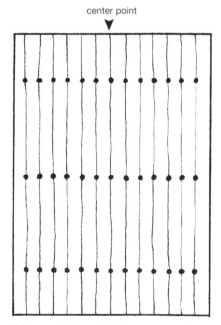

center point

Make a sewing template from scrap card stock, with sewing holes marked.

Framed embossed artwork

Experimenting with handmade paper,

materials, and techniques may lead you to

create items of unique aesthetic value. Unusual

materials, put together in imaginative ways,

form the basis of real works of art that you

will be proud to display.

Frame selected papers and collages as an

inspirational gallery and a record of your

progress as a paper artist.

Materials
Sheets of handmade paper
Embossing materials (the pictured example
   uses pistachio shells)
Frame and foam core board backing to fit
Bamboo or twig
Linen thread

Tools
Papermaking and pressing apparatus
Craft knife or paper scissors
Needle
Hammer and framing nails
Framing tape (self-adhesive brown paper tape)
Picture hanging kit
Pins

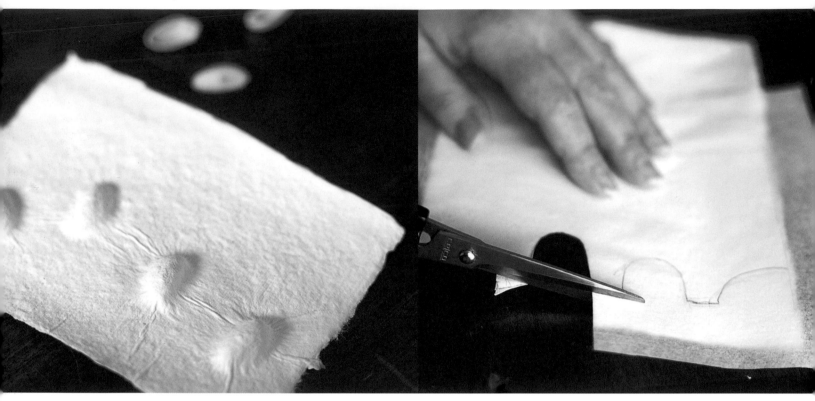

step two Emboss paper with pistachio shells.

step three Cut a second piece of paper to reveal the embossed design in the first.

1 Make several sheets of paper the required size. It may help to make the paper to fit a standard size frame. Cotton rag pulp gives a pleasing texture and recycled mount board is equally successful. Press the sheets gently between two boards. Do not dry.

2 Arrange embossing materials on a water-absorbent board: in this example, pistachio shells were used to create high, raised lumps in the paper. Place the wet, pressed paper carefully over the embossing material and gently press with a sponge. Leave to dry for at least 24 hours before you remove the embossing materials. See the basic instructions for embossing on page 27.

3 Use a sharp craft knife or paper scissors to cut a design in a second piece of paper, which will reveal the embossed parts of the first sheet. It is best to use a piece of tracing paper to work out your design before cutting into the handmade paper.

4 Hold the two pieces of paper firmly together. Fold over the extra paper at the top and stitch the two pages together with linen thread.

5 Use a piece of bamboo or another aesthetically pleasing twig to hang the work from, and stitch it on to the folded paper with linen thread.

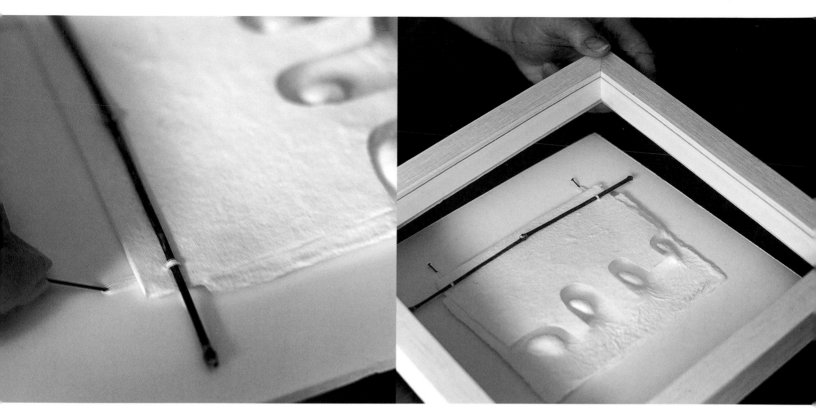

step six Make loops of linen thread and hang the artwork with pins.

step eight Insert the artwork in a box frame.

6 Make some loops with the linen thread, by which to hang the work in the frame. Using pins, secure the work to a foam core board backing, cut to fit inside the frame of your choice. When positioning the work, try to leave an equal amount of space around all sides.

7 You can purchase a box frame from a furniture store, art supplies store, or a framer. If your artwork is not a standard size, you may need to have a frame custom made. A framer can usually make small box frames economically from off cuts. Have the glass provided with spacers included. (Spacers are small pieces of card inserted between the frame and the glass so that the artwork does not touch the glass.)

8 Insert the artwork into the frame and secure the foam core board backing by hammering in very fine framing nails. Cover the gaps between the edges of the frame and the edges of the backing board with self-adhesive brown paper tape, available from a hardware or art supplies store.

9 Picture hanging kits may be purchased from hardware stores, art suppliers, and framers. Screw eyelets or D-rings into the back of the frame and add wire or cord for hanging at the desired height.

Wall hanging

For centuries wall hangings, particularly tapestries, have provided attractive artifacts to adorn walls. Not everyone can afford tapestries, but paper provides an inexpensive and aesthetically pleasing medium to create an artwork for the home or office without the necessity of expensive framing.

This wall hanging employs the technique of laminating two sheets of paper together with embroidery threads layered between the two sheets. Alternative designs might use raffia or string for a more rustic look, or cord to create more defined embossing. Ferns or flowers can also be included and you could consider allowing the threads to extend beyond the bottom sheets of paper, adding buttons, beads, or shells to give weight and add interest.

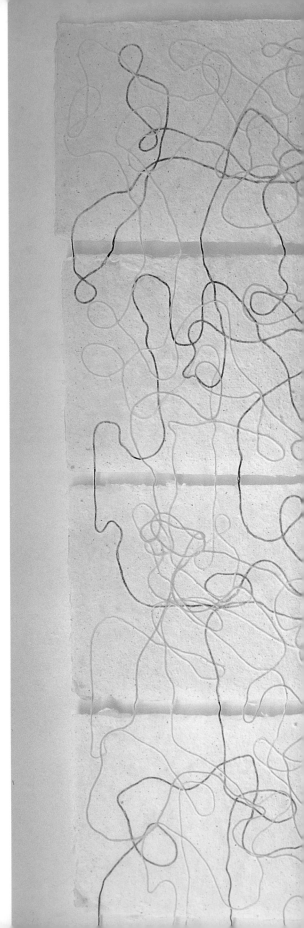

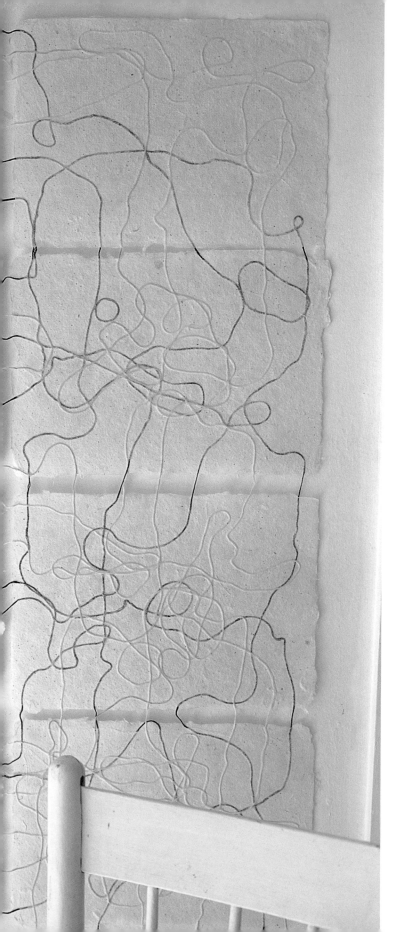

Materials

Pulp from any fiber paper that tends to
transparency, such as kozo or flax
Embroidery threads and any other items to
layer between the two sheets of paper
Wooden or metal rod (to hang)
Repositionable poster putty

Tools

Papermaking equipment and pressing
apparatus
Large sheet of paper for template
Large sheet of glass or transparent plastic

step one Lay a large sheet of clear glass or plastic over the template.

step three Transfer the sheets from the couching cloth to the glass or plastic sheet, aligning carefully.

1 Draw up a template on a large piece of paper to indicate the position of each sheet of paper that will form the first layer. This wall hanging comprises six legal-size sheets in landscape orientation. Place a sheet of glass or transparent plastic over the template drawing and tape it down firmly to the table.

2 Make the required number of sheets of paper for the first layer of the wall hanging. These sheets should be of medium weight. Press the sheets to remove excess water.

3 Hold each newly formed sheet of paper on the couching cloth and position each one on the template. Roll with a paint roller to ensure the sheet of paper is smooth and securely fixed to the glass or plastic sheeting.

4 Add the inclusions. Scatter the embroidery threads over the sheets, ensuring that they cross the gaps between sheets where possible. This is what holds the wall hanging together, so make sure there are plenty of connections. Leave enough lengths of thread at the top of the wall hanging to tie to a wooden or metal rod. When you are happy with the arrangement of threads, roll over the pages with a paint roller to press.

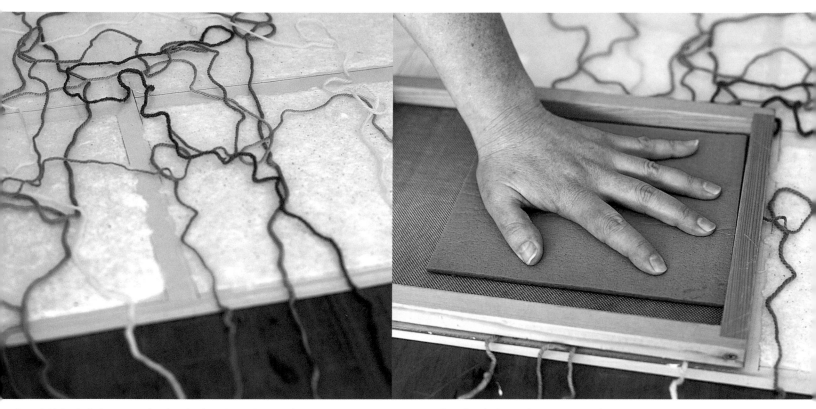

step four Add the inclusions, ensuring that the threads overlap the sheets.

step five Couch the top layers on top and remove excess water with a sponge.

5 If necessary, add extra water to the vat to ensure that the sheets for the top layer will be very fine. Make one sheet at a time and couch each sheet separately onto one of the bottom layers of paper. This should be done while the bottom sheet is still wet. Before you remove the mold, soak up excess water by placing a sponge on the mesh of the mold and pressing firmly to remove the excess water. The pressure will help to laminate the top sheet to the bottom sheet and the mold should lift off easily, leaving the newly formed top sheet adhered to the bottom sheet. Roll over the sheets again with the paint roller. This will give the effect of embossing.

6 Leave the wet wall hanging in position on the glass or plastic sheet until it is completely dry.

7 When dry, lift the sheets carefully from the surface and tie the threads around a timber or metal rod. Tie a cord to each end of the rod to allow the hanging to be suspended on the wall. Alternatively, affix the wall hanging with repositionable poster putty.

Hints

The wall hanging shown here was made with kozo paper. The first layer was of medium weight and, after addition of the threads, a very fine layer of kozo was added on top. The fine layer is almost transparent and it allows the inclusions to show through. The same effect can be achieved by using fine Japanese rice paper. Coat the first layer of paper with paste (see recipe on page 53) and add inclusions before placing the top layer.

Index

Thunder Bay Press

An imprint of the Advantage Publishers Group
5880 Oberlin Drive, San Diego, CA 92121-4794
www.thunderbaybooks.com

ISBN-13: 978-1-59223-691-6
ISBN-10: 1-59223-691-X

Library of Congress Cataloging-in-Publication data available upon request

Design concept: Tracey Loughlin
Art direction: Vivien Valk
Designer: Jacqueline Richards
Project manager: Janine Flew
Editor: Melody Lord
Diagrams and templates: Amanda McKittrick, Heather Menzies
Photographer: Natasha Milne
Stylist: Sarah O'Brien
Production: Monika Paratore
Project designers, makers and writers (Primrose Paper Arts Inc): Jeanette Bakker (Laminated paper
folder, Stick book, Double concertina with paper cutouts, Torn book, Small chunky collage book,
simple sewn books pictured on page 85); Jill Elias (Basic recycled paper, Inclusions and variations,
Star book, Concertina card holder, Japanese-style stitched books); Helen Roberts Hill (Framed embossed
artwork); Jean Riley (Envelopes, including those pictured on page 7, Fan card, Handmade books,
Eight-fold concertina book, Cover options, Interlocking concertina book, Photo album, Simple sewn
books, Wall hanging); Marie Waterhouse (Plant fiber papers, Laminating, Embedding, Embossing,
Trifold card, Stationery folder)

Printed in China by 1010 Printing International Limited
1 2 3 4 5 10 09 08 07 06